I0162695

Hannah Whitall Smith

The Feminist Connections of a Holiness Icon

Twenty Women Leaders of the 19th Century and Their Connections to Hannah Whitall Smith

Written and Edited By

Robert A. Danielson

Table of Contents

Introducting Hannah

"My first introduction to fanaticism, if I leave out all that I got from the Quakers to start with, which was a good deal, came through the Methodist doctrine of entire sanctification. That doctrine has been one of the greatest blessings of my life, but it has also introduced me into an emotional region where common sense has no chance, and where everything goes by feelings and voices and impressions."

-Hannah Whitall Smith

From her introduction to the Overcomers and Anna Spafford (chapter six) in *Religious Fanaticism: Extracts from the Papers of Hannah Whitall Smith*, edited with an introduction by Ray Strachey, published by Faber & Gwyer Limited (1928), page 203.

Hannah Whitall Smith (Feb. 7, 1832-May 1, 1911)
(Image from the Archives of the B.L. Fisher Library)

Introduction

One of the unexpected results of the Holiness Movement was a rise in the empowerment of Christian women, and the fact that this empowerment was not just relegated to the spiritual dimensions of life. It spread into social, political, and other public arenas. It is possible to trace this emergence back to Phoebe Palmer (Dec. 18, 1807-Nov. 2, 1874) and her strong role in the founding of the movement through a reinterpretation of John Wesley and John Fletcher's views of sanctification. As Briane Turley (1999:50) quotes in his book, *A Wheel Within a Wheel: Southern Methodism and the Georgia Holiness Association*, "Historian Nancy Cott has observed that women's prayerful contact with God enabled them 'to assert themselves, both in private and public ways.' Moreover, this contact with the transcendent helped them 'to rely on an authority beyond the world of men and provided a crucial support to those who stepped beyond accepted bounds.'"

Since Phoebe Palmer argued the empowerment and blessing of God through the Holy Spirit had greater authority than cultural and religious traditions that kept women from teaching and other positions of spiritual leadership, this understanding among Holiness women began to expand outside of purely religious circles. As Susie Stanley (1989:115) notes, "Wesleyan/Holiness women preachers directly challenged the doctrine of domesticity by extending their calling outside the home. Likewise, temperance women, relying on the power of the Holy Spirit, spoke in public and attacked the evils of alcohol. Empowered by the Holy Spirit, they moved outside the home to fulfill their calling."

The Temperance Movement was perhaps the first political and social force to emerge from the empowerment of Holiness women. It tied itself clearly to a moral issue with strong support within the Holiness world. It was an issue that had a clear impact on the family and the family's finances. Women who could prevent husbands from turning to alcohol felt they could have more stable and secure homes. Yet, as women because empowered in the Temperance Movement, they also realized the success involved in motivating armies of women for social change. It is almost directly from the Temperance Movement that the Suffrage Movement and other women-led attempts for social change began to emerge.

This move can perhaps be best seen in the life and relationships of Hannah Whitall Smith (Feb. 7, 1832-May 1, 1911). Perhaps best known as the writer of the Holiness classic *The Christian's Secret to a Happy Life*, this Quaker from Pennsylvania and her husband, Robert Pearsall Smith, were very much influenced by William E. Boardman and became leaders in the Holiness Movement in The United States and the Higher Life Movement in Great Britain. Hannah quickly outshone her husband in speaking and she carried on an extensive correspondence with many people, but especially women both within and outside of these movements.

Hannah Whitall Smith built off of her sanctification experience to become involved in other movements that empowered women. In 1874 she helped found the Women's Christian Temperance Union, and soon became good friends with its second president, Frances Willard. Willard had holiness roots going back to Oberlin College, and she was a devout Methodist her entire life. Hannah would serve a number of offices in the W.C.T.U., but was most known in her office as Secretary of Evangelism for the W.C.T.U.

It was from her Temperance connections that Hannah Whitall Smith became involved in the Suffrage Movement. In 1888, the Women's International Council was held in Washington D.C. with representatives from 53 women's organizations in nine countries coming together to form what would become the International Council of Women. Both Frances Willard and Hannah Whitall Smith were present for this meeting which was organized by prominent women interested in helping women get the right to vote. The leaders included Susan B. Anthony and Elizabeth Cady Stanton.

In many ways it was a natural progression to move from Temperance work, where Hannah could see the political and moral power of women in action to seeing the injustice of not allowing women to vote for political leaders or against unjust laws. From her involvement with the Women's Temperance and Suffrage Movements, Hannah began to connect with other social movements lead by women in the United States and in England. Frances Power Cobbe and her anti-vivisection movement for animal welfare was one such movement, and so was her interest in the work of Josephine Butler, who fought against sex slave traffic in Europe and against laws that marginalized and oppressed prostitutes in Britain.

Hannah's rich correspondence connected her with all kinds of women who were active in various ways in her time, from Anna Spafford, the leader of a small cult in Jerusalem and Amelia Stone Quinton, who fought for the civil rights of Native Americans to Clara Barton of the American Red Cross and Ellice Hopkins, co-founder of the White Cross Army, which was a sexual purity movement among men. But she also connected with more marginalized women, such as Constance Holland, the wife of Oscar Wilde after his public sexual scandals, and Olive Schreiner, South Africa's first novelist, who opposed racism in her works.

Examining the connections between women of the Holiness Movement is not always easy. Often they are underrepresented in history and may be only occasionally referenced in official accounts of the time. Nevertheless, there arise fascinating connections, such as Hannah's friendship with spiritualists, Lord and Lady Mount-Temple in Great Britain, who sponsored the Broadlands Conference, which also brought African-American evangelist, Amanda Smith (another friend of Hannah's) to speak to early meetings of the Higher Life Movement. Hannah also played a vital role in connecting Lady Isabella Somerset (a president of the British Women's Temperance Movement) with Frances Willard (of the World's Women Christian Temperance Association).

While many of the issues important to the women Hannah corresponded with cannot be considered "Holiness" issues, her moral authority through the impact of *The Christian's Secret to a Happy Life* seems to have made a major impression. Many of the women were not part of the Holiness Mc ovement, and Hannah did not mind moving in very different circles. Yet, her empowerment to speak as a sanctified Quaker in both the issues of temperance and suffrage, helped empower other generations of women outside of the Holiness Movement to speak for a wide variety of social and political causes.

A thorough study of the correspondence found in the Papers of Hannah Whitall Smith in the Special Collections of Asbury Theological Seminary reveal just how interconnected this Holiness leader was with a plethora of women working on many issues affecting women in her time and day. This exhibit, attempts to categorize some of these issues in five general categories: Religious Revival, Social Change, Political Activism, Cultural Transformation, and Civil Rights. Under each category are four key examples of women connected to Hannah Whitall Smith, most often through correspondence, and a sample letter is included. In many cases, these women could fall under several of these categories, but for purposes of this exhibit we have attempted to categorize them to emphasize the broad nature of women's movements of this time.

Part One: Religious Revival

"How strange and unwarrantable, the infatuation of some who professed to be Christ's disciples of the present day, who contemptuously hear 'the testimony of Jesus, which is the spirit of prophesy,' because it falls from the lips of a woman!"

-Phoebe Palmer

Promise of the Father, or, A neglected specialty of the last days: addressed to the clergy and laity of all Christian Communities (1859) page 17.

Emelia Gurney (1823-1896)
(Image in the Public Domain)

Biography

Emilia Russell Gurney (Batten) (July 26, 1823-1896) was born into an Anglican family with ministers on both sides of her family. Her maternal grandfather was John Venn of the Clapham Sect, an Anglican group of social reformers founded by John Newton and closely associated with William Wilberforce. They were closely involved in political movements for the abolition of the slave trade and the abolition of slavery in Britain. In 1852, Emelia married Russell Gurney and they moved to Kensington Park Gardens.

Emelia Gurney became one of the founders of the Kensington Society from 1865-1868. This group of feminists, reformers, and suffragists met on a regular basis and submitted topics for discussion. It was an environment where women were free to discuss and debate political and social issues. A number of the founding members went on to become key women in various social movements. They included Sarah Emily Davies who was a pioneering campaigner for women's access to university, Barbara Bodichon and Jessie Boucherett who founded the Society for Promoting the Employment of Women, Elizabeth Garrett Anderson who was the first woman in Britain to qualify as a physician and surgeon, and Rosamond Davenport Hill who was a noted prison reformer.

Together the Kensington Society petitioned parliament for women's rights to vote. After this petition failed they became the London National Society for Women's Suffrage, then the National Society for Women's Suffrage and finally the National Union of Women's Suffrage Societies. As such a played it crucial role in the work to achieve the right for women to vote in Britain.

Emilia's husband, Russell, served in parliament where he advocated for women's issues including the Married Women's Property Act of 1870 and the UK Medical Acts of 1876, which permitted women to become physicians and surgeons. Emilia was also a member of the Mount Temple religious circle sponsored by Baron Mount Temple and his wife, Georgina. She attended the Broadlands Conferences from 1874-1888, where she became a close associate of Hannah Whitall Smith.

3, ORME SQUARE.

IX 13
18 86
W.

Give true love
to her beloved
Mrs Beck - her
meet in silence.
Many waters cannot
quench love. Neither
can the floods drown
it - How man w?
Give all the substance
of his house for love
it it. utterly be
contemned + to
think thou hast freely given

Beloved Sister Hannah

What an event
it is in one's life & get
such a love letter as thine
lying just now before me!
I often think, notwithstanding
a certain Divine parsimony
& holding back that at
times one seems to perceive
& suffer under, that there
is also a tropical abundance

Beloved Sister Hannah,

What an event it is in ones life to get such a love letter as thine lying just now before me! I often think, notwithstanding a certain Divine parsimony and holding back that at times one seems to perceive and suffer under, that there is also a tropical abundance

that no out stretched arms
can receive — & as one
has no absolute standard
or measure as to fullness
or emptiness one fails
to grasps the idea first
of one & then of the other
tho no doubt God gives
ever more far more
than one can receive —
This is such a special
day for me to get such
a blessed thing as thy

me thine — Praise the Lord Oh my soul! — Thine E. RS.

that no outstretched arms can receive — and
as one has no absolute standard or measure
as to fullness or emptiness one grasps the idea
first of one and then of the other though
no doubt God gives ever more far more than
one can receive. This is such a special day
for me to get such a blessed thing as thy

letter - because it is the
never to be fogotten anni
versary of that heaven -
opening that came to me
through thy & thy husbands
ministrations 12 years
ago - a bridal day
between Heaven & Earth
that my eyes were opened
to behold when I saw
the sap of Lonelife moving
in the Cipple tree & felt
it in my own veins &
heard the meaning of the

letter—because it is the never to be forgotten anniversary of that heaven opening that came to me through thy and thy husband's ministrations 12 years ago—a bridal day between Heaven and Earth that my eyes were opened to behold when I saw the sap of Lovelife moving in the Apple tree and felt it in my own veins and heard the meaning of the

Word Immanuel — To
have a token of unity
with the teaching of that
time, thee may well
fancy is unutterably sweet —
& truly I must take
up my bed & walk
I think with such a
message as thou sendest
me — Darling — I am
much better — nothing
did me good till this
day week When my old
Dr returning, he treated
me for rheumatic gout —

word _Immanuel_ — To have a token of unity
with the teaching of that time. thee may
well fancy is unutterably sweet and truly
I must take up my bed and walk I think
with such a message as thou sendest me.

Darling — I am much better — nothing did
me good till this day week when my old Dr.
returning, he treated me for _rheumatic gout_

2/ in my jaw — since then
that worst pain of
vitriol slowly passing
through & in all my teeth
skinning them to my very
soul! has not repeated
itself. There was a kind
of fiendish deliberate action
about it — that really wounded
my sentimental part!
My Dr. says this kind of
attack seldom departs
under 6 weeks — the blood
has poison in it & cant
get free of it — It is
strange tho' to me, thy dear
feeling that pain & I should

in my jaw— since then that worst pain of
vitriol slowly passing through and in all
my teeth skinning them to my very soul
has not defeated itself. There was a kind
of fiendish deliberate action about it—that
really wounded my sentimental part! My
Dr. says this kind of attack seldom departs
under 6 weeks—the blood has poison in it and
can't get free of it—It is strange though to
me, thy dear feeling that pain and I should

not become intimates.
On the contrary I have
long felt that there was
a certain callousness about
me that only by such
discipline I be cut out.
but I know nothing
but am known of God.
What words — do I,
can I believe them? —
Sometimes by flashes — ʌ
in those flashes I will fain
live — The Lodge
has been here — suffering
too & yet reading to me

not become intimates. On the contrary I have long felt that there was a certain callowness about me that only by such discipline could be cut out, but I know nothing but am known of God. What words—do I, can I believe them? Sometimes by flashes—and in those flashes I would fain live.

The Lady has been here—suffering too and yet reading to me

beautiful exalted words
by our Archbishop — I
said I will try & go to
night if only for half
an hour — but I seem
to be told not — I took
my farewell glance of
my strong Sister–Mother
Hannah & hardly feel
as if I could grapple
with saying Goodbye
again — Uniter sent
me thy Secret & I read
it thro' on Sunday with
glad consent to every

beautiful exalted words by our Archbishop—
I said I would try and go tonight if only
for half an hour— but I seem to be be told
not—I took my farewell glance of my strong
Sister—other Hannah and hardly feel as if
I could grapple with saying goodbye again.
Uniter sent me thy Secret and I read it
through on Sunday with glad consent to every

Word & an intention to
take some day by day
for daily bread — The
"Although" & "Yet" chapter
I read to my invalids &
found them drinking it
in — That verse (Hab/ my
blessed Mr Erskine used
to repeat & re-repeat with
persevering delight —
Did you ever read his
life? — if not, I must
send it you — I have
written on & on because
on board ship you will
have time to read how anything

word and an intention to take some day by day for daily bread. The "Although" and "Yet" chapters I read to my invalids and found them drinking it in. That verse (Hab) my blessed W. Erskine used to repeat and re-repeat with persevering delight. Did you ever read his life? — if not, I must send it to you. I have written on and on because on board ship you will have time to read anything.

(The rest of the letter is found on pgs. 1-2 written sideways)

Give true love to ever beloved J.W. Beck— we meet in silence. Many waters cannot quench love, neither can the floods drown it. — If a man would give all the substance of his house for love, it would utterly be condemned— and to think thou hast freely given me thine! Praise the Lord Oh my soul!

Thine,

E.R.G.

(Emilia Russell Gurney)

Margaret Bottome (Dec. 29, 1827- Nov. 14, 1906)
(Image in the author's collection)

Biography

Margaret McDonald Bottome (Dec. 29, 1827-Nov. 14, 1906) was a religious leader born and raised in New York City. Her father died in 1852, leaving his widow and eighteen children. Margaret was the eldest and had just gotten married to a Methodist preacher, Rev. Frank Bottome. She remained a devout Methodist, as did many of her siblings, throughout her life.

After giving informal talks on the Bible to women, she along with a group of nine other women formed a permanent group in 1886. This group focused on Bible study and Christian service to others, and they named themselves "Kings Daughters." Each of the women formed a group of ten, and those women did the same. By 1887 men had joined the movement, which eventually became the International Order of the King's Daughters and Sons. She wrote a column for the *Ladies Home Journal* called "Heart to Heart Talks." Her books include: *Our Lord's Seven Questions After Easter* (1889), *Crumbs from the King's Table* (1894), and *Death and Life* (1897).

The International Order of the King's Daughters and Sons still exists, headquartered in Chautauqua, New York. There various "circles" have been active in supporting ministry scholarships, thrift stores, hospitals, homes for the elderly, and child care centers. They have also supported Native American ministries since 1934.

about Dowie

HEADQUARTERS OF THE
INTERNATIONAL ORDER OF
THE KING'S DAUGHTERS AND SONS
156 FIFTH AVENUE

MRS. MARGARET BOTTOME, PRES.
MISS KATE BOND, VICE-PRES.
MRS. MARY LOWE DICKINSON, GEN. SEC'Y AND EDITOR
MRS. ISABELLA CHARLES DAVIS, COR. SEC'Y AND TREAS.
MRS. A. H. EVANS, REC. SEC'Y.

NEW YORK, _Nov._ 1903

New York
Nov. 1903

It was such a torrid fizzle—his language was frightful calling people Skunk. Pol's. etc. etc—he missed such an opportunity for really the attitude of the best people was if he can do any good we bid him welcome. but I never saw anything like it— it seemed as if he was led of Satan—his followers were to be pitied. They were really respectable people—all did what they could, but he has injured himself in their sight. He was so dreadful in regard to the press that of course they turned on him. I would not have been in that Madison Ave. Garden, not for anything. He made no converts—did nothing but injure his cause. He is lingering here a few days, but no attention is being paid to him. I started off in sending you the papers but I must have sent them to Melie if you could not get them — The last experiment has been the death of Mrs Booth Tucker of the Salvation Army — was killed in a railway accident a few days ago, and such a dreadful mistake was made at the funeral. I do not know where the real right or the real wrong doth lie — they brought up the separations of the family again and her own brother Ballington Booth did not attend the funeral of his own sister. Such a pitiful picture before the world and outside of Church. He questions however arise in thy Christianity — O Hannah God is long suffering and of tender mercy — I am so sorry I have to send off this miserable little letter to you when I meant to have written something so different if you did not get them.

The last excitement has been the death of Mrs. Booth Tucker of the Salvation Army — was killed in a railway accident a few days ago, and such a dreadful mistake was made at the funeral. I do not know where the real right or the real wrong doth lie, but it brought up the separations of the family again, and her own brother Ballington Booth did not attend the funeral of his own sister, such a pitiful picture before the inside and outside at Church. The question would arise " is that Christianity? "

O Hannah, God is longsuffering and of tender mercy.

I am so sorry I have to send off this miserable little letter to you when I mean to have written something so different but I send lots of love.

Yours dutifully,

Thy M. Bottome
(Margaret Bottome)

Note: A note on this partial letter indicates that the subject mentioned at the beginning is John Alexander Dowie, a Scottish faith healer who claimed to be "Elijah the Restorer" to announce the second return of Christ. He built a large following in Chicago, near where he also established his utopian headquarters in the city of Zion. On Oct. 18, 1903, he brought his evangelists on a crusade to convert New York City, where he rented out Madison Square Gardens for two weeks. The event was a colossal failure for his Christian Catholic Church, which ultimately led to him being deposed and fleeing abroad to avoid his creditors.

Emma Moss Booth-Tucker was the fourth child of Catherine and William Booth. She and her husband were posted to the Salvation Army in the U.S. in 1896, after her brother Ballington and his wife Maud left the Salvation Army rather than be reassigned abroad. Ballington and his wife started Volunteers of America along the same lines as the Salvation Army.

Lady Georgina Mount-Temple (1822-1901)
(Image in the Public Domain)

Biography

Georgina Cowper-Temple (Tollemache) (1822-Oct. 17, 1901) was one of nine daughters of Admiral John Richard Delap Tollemache, who along with their three brothers were raised in Surrey. She married William Cowper-Temple on November 21, 1848 and was his second wife, later to become Lord and Lady Mount Temple. William would serve as private secretary to Lord Melbourne when he was Prime Minister and serve as a minister in the government of Lord Palmerston. Georgina became a major supporter of social reforms and formed friendships covering a wide spectrum of people. William inherited the Broadlands estate in Romsey in 1868.

The Mount Temples were very interested in religious matters and were friends with a number of Evangelical leaders, but they also formed friendships with unorthodox Christians, and had a particularly strong interest in spiritualism. All of this they saw as their way of searching for truth. But their main contribution was an annual ecumenical conference, which they would hold at their Broadlands estate from 1874 to 1888. It was here that William Boardman, Robert Pearsall Smith, and Hannah Whitall Smith would introduce and spread the holiness message, leading to the formation of the Deeper Life Movement in Britain. The Broadlands Conferences were not just for orthodox Christians or the Holiness Movement, and one might also encounter Hindus and mediums as well, however the Keswick Conventions emerged out of the Broadlands Conference to become a more representative holiness movement.

Georgina Mount Temple would remain a close friend of Hannah Whitall Smith, and as such became involved in the Temperance Movement. However, she was also a leader in the Torquay Anti-Vivisection Society and in the Royal Society for the Prevention of Cruelty to Animals. It is likely that Hannah was able to meet such a wide range of Victorian society through her close relationship to Lady Mount Temple.

Torquay. Devon,
Monday. Sep. 24 1877

Beloved Hannah. our dear _Angel
of the churches_. I must scribble a
little note to enclose in my letter
to Sister Sarah. feeling my heart
just overflowing with the love that
these Torn things cause to well up
in it deepest sources towards you—
own darling. How sorry these
unchristlike christians will be one
day. when their cruel conduct is
revealed to them — How they will
fall at your feet and beg the pardon
your generous heart will so freely
give. Dear One we [...] her have
[...] of times for their Holy Husband

Torquay. Devon
Monday. Sept. 24. 1877

Beloved Hannah. our dear Angel
of the Churches. I must scribble a
little line to enclose in my letter.

To Sister Sarah—feeling my head just
overflowing with the love that these sore
trials cause to well up in its deepest source
towards you—oh my darling. How sorry
these unChristlike Christians will be one day
when their cruel conduct is revealed to them
— How they will fall about your feet and
beg the pardon your generous heart will so
freely give. Dear one. the furnace has been
heated 7 times for thee and thy husband

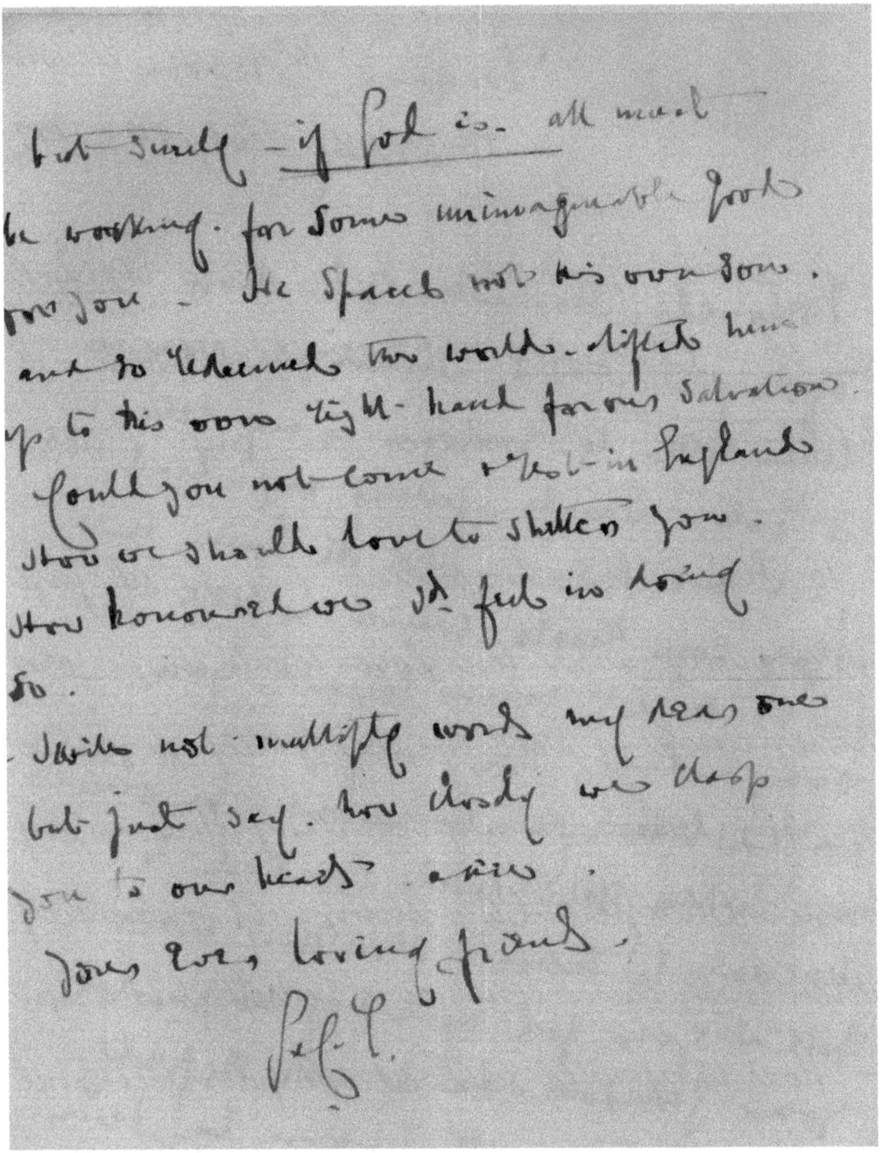

but surely — if God is — all must
be working for some unimaginable good
for you — He spared not his own Son,
and so redeemed the world — lifted him
up to his own right hand for our salvation.
Could you not come & rest in England
How we should love to shelter you.
How honoured we sh^d feel in doing
so.
I write not — multiply words my dear one
but just say, how closely we clasp
you to our hearts — anew.
Yours ever, loving friend.

but surely — *if God is* all must be working for some unimaginable good for you. He spared not his own son and so redeemed the world, lifted him up to his own right hand for our salvation.

Could you not come rest in England? How we should love to shelter you. How honored we would feel in doing so.

I will not multiply words my dear one, but just say how closely we clasp you to our heart anew.

Your ever—loving friend,

G.C.T.
(Georgina Cowper—Temple)

Note: We are unsure who is referenced as "Sister Sarah" or what trials she is referring to, but the letter gives a good feel for the ecumenical (if not completely orthodox) spirit of Lady Mount Temple and her religious nature. This letter also uses the term sometimes applied to Hannah as "The Angel of the Churches."

Frances Ridley Havergal (Dec. 14, 1836-June 3, 1879)
(Image in the Public Domain)

Biography

Frances Ridley Havergal (Dec. 14, 1836-June 3, 1879) was born into the family of an Anglican clergyman and except for a short time studying and traveling in Germany and Switzerland; she remained at home, frequently in ill health. She did not marry or have children and she died at the young age of 42 years old. She wrote religious poetry, hymns, tracts, and some literature for children, most of which was published after her death by her sisters.

This powerful letter recounts her experience of sanctification, which she credits in part to the work of Robert Pearsall Smith and Hannah Whitall Smith. Her most famous hymn, "Take My Life and Let it Be" became a powerful hymn in both holiness and missionary circles, and as such influenced thousands of Christians throughout the last century.

Take my life and let it be consecrated, Lord, to Thee.
Take my moments and my days; let them flow in ceaseless praise.
Take my hands, and let them move at the impulse of thy love.
Take my feet, and let them be swift and beautiful for thee.

Take my voice, and let me sing always, only, for my King.
Take my lips, and let them be filled with messages from thee.
Take my silver and my gold; not a mite would I withhold.
Take my intellect, and use every power as thou shalt choose.

Take my will, and make it thine; it shall be no longer mine.
Take my heart, it is thine own; it shall be thy royal throne.
Take my love, my Lord, I pour at thy feet its treasure store.
Take myself, and I will be ever, only, all for thee.

43. Binswood Avenue, Leamington.
(From Frances Ridley Havergall
author of "This have I done for thee" &c.) Oct. 18. 1875.

Dear Mrs Smith

I must send a line of thanks
for your dear husband's kind note to me,
but it shall be through you, in case
he is not well enough to be teased
with letters. It seems to me the first
& easiest lesson to cast one's own care on
the Lord, but a harder one to leave
one's friends & their matters in His hands,
& hardest of all to trust Him about
His own affairs! And so, while it is
long since I had the least ripple of
care about anything to do with myself,
I have, until quite lately, failed to
learn the other two lessons, & the
Master has made use of you, (i.e both
of you, I mean) & that part of His cause
of which you are the champions, to shew
me the failure & teach me the lessons!
O how I have been vexing & chafing
over the prejudice & opposition & false
witness, & how I have been mourning
because so many who she have been
helping were hindering (apparently)
the Lord's own work! And how I have
wanted to explode & speak my mind!

43 Briarwood Avenue, Leamington
Oct. 18. 1875

Dear Mrs. Smith

I just want to send a line of thanks for your dear
husband's kind note to me, but it shall be through <u>you</u>,
in case he is not well enough to be tended with letters.
It seems to me the first and easiest lesson to cast one's
own care on the Lord, but a harder one to leave one's
friends and <u>their</u> matters in His hands, and hardest of
all to trust Him about His own affairs! And so, while
it is long since I had the least ripple of care about
anything to do with myself. I have until quite lately,
failed to learn the other two lessons, and the Master
has made use of you (i.e. <u>both</u> of you, I mean) and
that part of His cause of which you are the champions,
to <u>shew</u> me the failure and teach me the lessons! Oh,
how I have been vexing and chafing over the prejudice
and opposition and false witness and how I have been
mourning because so many who should have been helping
were hindering (apparently) the Lord's own work!
And how I have wanted to explode and speak my mind!

Well, it is all over now — the saintly silence of R. P. S. & H. W. S. has shown me a more excellent way, and at last I have seen how foolish and sinful it was not to leave your affairs and His affairs as entirely & restfully to Him as my own. Oh I am so thankful for this place of silence given to you, for I believe the eloquence of its is gradually & surely resounding, & witnessing for the truth of God as no defence of yourselves could possibly do. Just as if He would not vindicate His own witnesses! And just as if the Enemy could prevail against His truth! I am so glad He has taught me at last to trust Him entirely in all this matter. — I did not know there was such a gap in my armour. One good must have at once resulted from Mr Smith's illness — I suppose thousands more prayers went up for him than if he had been kept in health — when I heard of it I really felt inclined to congratulate him! for I knew how the hearts of God's people would be stirred up to pray for him. And I knew a little, too, of how tenderly gracious the Master

Well it is all over now—the _saintly silence_ of R.P.S. and H.W.S. has shown me a more excellent way, and at last I have seen how foolish and sinful it was to leave _your_ affairs and _His_ affairs as entirely and restfully to Him as my own. Oh, I am so thankful for this grace of silence given to you, for I believe the eloquence of it is gradually and surely resounding and witnessing for the truth of God as no defense of yourselves could possibly do. Just as if He would not vindicate His own witnesses! And just as if the Enemy _could_ prevail against His truth! I am so glad He has taught me at last to trust Him entirely in all this matter—I did not know there was such a gap in my armour.

One good must have at once resulted from Mr. Smith's illness—I suppose _thousands more_ prayers went up for him than if he had been kept in health—when I heard of it I really felt inclined to congratulate him! For I knew how the hearts of God's people would be stirred up to pray for him. And I knew a little too, of how tenderly gracious the Master

Himself would be to him, & what praise
he would be sure to have to give for
this unexpected "calling apart." For myself, I don't know how to thank God
enough for my own illness, it is a retrospect of unmingled praise. I cannot
imagine why He is so very good to me,
having no mysteries in His dealings
with me, but letting me see a mar-
vellous array of wonderfully wise reasons
why He did just as He did with me,
& why it was just at that time. From
the very day I trusted myself wholly
to Him, He has always let me see
this clearly in everything. I hardly know how to
express, but I think you will understand me if I say that, though continually testing my trust in a singular variety of ways, He never yet
(these two years) seems to have tried
it so that I shall be conscious of any
strain upon it; - I entrusted it to Him
& He so keeps it, that in every test however severe
it has been as if He almost changed
the faith into very sight while the
testing lasted. I want to tell every
one who shrinks from illness & pain that

Himself would be to him, and what praise he would be
sure to have to give for this unexpected "calling apart."
For myself, I don't know how to thank God enough for
my own illness, it is a retrospect of unmingled praise.
I cannot imagine why He is so very good to me, having
no _mysteries_ in His dealings with me, but letting me
see a marvelous array of wonderfully wise reasons _why_
He did just as He did with me, and _why_ it was just
at that time. From the very day I trusted myself
wholly to Him, He has _always_ let me see thus clearly
in everything—I hardly know how to express, but I
think you will understand me if I say that through
continually _testing_ my trust in a singular variety of
ways, He never yet (these two years) seems to have _tried_
it so that I shall be conscious of any strain upon it; I
entrusted it to Him, and He _so_ keeps it, that in every
test however _severe_ it has been as if He almost changed
the faith into my _sight_ while the testing lasted. I want
to tell every one who shrinks from illness and pain that

they really need "fear no evil." I
am pretty well now, but not at all
strong, & I do not somehow think it
likely I ever shall be — I was by no
means strong before my illness, but
I am considerable below my former
level — a very little extra talking or
walking knocks me up for days. I
have been delighting in thinking that
we can re-enact the miracle of the loaves
& fishes as to our work — that His blessing can make a few words feed
many thousands, & multiply one hour's,
nay, one minute's work, if He will,
to the value of weeks or years of effort
& labour. And even supposing one
could not do anything at all again
on earth, one might well acquiesce
in a lifetime of passive moulding
& mellowing for the grand service
of eternity — for the Master's use
above. You asked me, more than a year
ago to tell you "whether I had been
for any length of time consecrated
before realising union with Jesus" or
words to that effect. I could not
answer then because I was taken ill. I

they _really_ need "fear no evil."

I am pretty _well_ now, but not at all strong, and I do not somehow think it likely I ever shall be. I was by not means strong before my illness, but I am considerably below my former level, a _very_ little exter talking or walking knocks me up for days. I have been delighting in thinking that He can re-enact the miracle of the loaves and fishes as to our _work_—that His blessings can make a few words feed many thousands and multiples one hour's way, one _minute's_ work, if He will to the value of weeks or years of effort of labor. And even supposing one could not do anything _at all_ again on earth, one might well acquiesce in a lifetime of passive molding and meetening for the proud service of eternity—for the Master's use above.

You asked me more than a year ago to tell you "whether I had been for any length of time consecrated before realizing union with Jesus" or words to that effect. I could not answer then because I was taken ill. I think not. For some 2 or 3 years I had been more desirous to "follow fully", & had practically given more & more of love & time & strength to Christ, but consecration as a "definite transaction" had never been brought before me. – I did not know the real meaning of my own words "full & glad surrender", & of what "deliverance from sin" might mean, I had no notion. I had been a long, long time learning to realize justification, & lately had gone on from that to entering into the comforting & praise-awakening doctrines of God's "sovereign grace in election & final perseverance", & from this platform I worked for more happily & successfully among others. I wondered what He would teach me next, having been very conscious of progressive teaching. Then came what M.Smith told me he calls "conviction for holiness" some weeks of utter dissatisfaction & craving for I hardly knew what, then three days of seeing what I wanted, & tremendous turmoil of soul about it. Then – just think _not_. For some 2 or 3 years I had been more desirous to "follow fully" and had _practically_ given more and more of _love_ and time and strength to Christ. but consecration as a "_definite_ transaction" had never been brought before me. I did not know the real meaning of my own words "full and glad surrender" and of what "deliverance from sin" might mean. I had no notion. I had been a long, long time learning to realize justification and latterly had gone on from that to entering into the comforting and praise awakening doctrines of God's sovereign grace in election and "final perseverance" and from this platform I worked far more happily and ~~successfully~~ among others. I wondered what He would teach me next. having been very conscious of progressive teaching.

Then came what Mr. Smith told me he calls "conviction for holiness" some weeks neither dissatisfaction or craving for I hardly knew what. then three days of seeing what I wanted and tremendous turmoil of soul about it. Then—just one sentence in a letter from Mr Stanford – "For conscious sin there is instant confession & instant forgiveness – for unconscious sin the blood of Christ [*cleanseth, i.e.*] goes on cleansing"! [*This was the message of deliverance to me!*] I really seemed as if I saw everything at once, just as you see a whole landscape in one flash where before you saw nothing! Everything which I have read or seen since, seemed there at once – consecration, definite, total, rapturous – then & there! trust, equally definite & entire, seemed a matter of course! the definite purpose to "sin no more" because the precious blood could & would go on cleansing, the instant vision, as clear as daylight, that every scrap of care was to be cast on Him, & every shred of unbelief renounced for ever – that He meant all He said, that no commands were impossible, no promises unattainable – all this seemed simultaneous! And no human teaching had anything whatever to do with it it was all new to me,

one sentence in a letter from Mr. Wrenford—"For conscious sin there is instant confession and instant forgiveness—for unconscious sin the blood of Christ <u>cleanseth</u>, i.e. <u>goes on</u> cleansing"! That was the message of <u>deliverance</u> to me! I really received as if I saw everything <u>at once</u>, just as you see a whole landscape in one flash where before you saw <u>nothing</u>! Everything which I have read or seen since seemed there at once—consecration, definite, total, rapturous— <u>then and there</u>! Trust equally definite and entire, seemed a <u>matter of course</u>! The definite purpose to "sin no more" <u>because</u> the precious blood could and would <u>go on</u> cleansing, the <u>instant</u> vision, as clear as daylight, that every scrap of care was to be cast on Him, and every shred of unbelief renounced for ever—that He meant <u>all</u> He said, that <u>no</u> commands were impossible, <u>no</u> promises unattainable—all this seemed simultaneous! And no human teaching had anything whatever to do with it— it was all <u>new</u> to me.

so what could it have been but the Spirit Himself teaching me! It was not till weeks after that I first read anything on the subject, and then I found it all in print! I am so exceedingly thankful that He taught me thus — that I have not the regret of having heard before accepting — of having hesitated to receive the full salvation, & delayed my surrender & trust. He sent the power with the first word of definite deliverance which had reached my ear or eye — so don't you think I have extra cause for praise! Others tell me of having read books & been to Conferences, & "known all about it ever so long", & then being taught to receive the teaching line by line, gradually, getting hold of it a little bit at a time; but to me it was as if He poured out more treasure into my lap at once than I have had time even to count yet! It is a strange contrast to all His previous teaching of me, it was peculiarly gradual. — I

so what could it have been but the Spirit Himself teaching me!

It was not till weeks after that I first read anything on the subject, and then I found it all in print! I am so exceedingly thankful that He taught me this—that I have not the regret of having heard before accepting—of having hesitated to receive the full salvation and delayed my surrender and trust. He sent the power with the first word of definite deliverance, which had reached my ear or eye—so don't you think I have extra cause for praise! Others tell me of having read books and been to Conferences, and "known all about it ever so long" and then being taught to receive the teaching line by line, gradually getting hold of it a little bit at a time; but to me it was as if He poured out more treasure into my lap at once than I have had time even to count yet! It is a strange contrast to all His previous teaching of me, which was peculiarly gradual. I

Note: Mr Wrenford refers to Rev. John Tinson Wrenford (1825-1904), a prolific Anglican writer and clergyman, who formed a close bond with Frances Havergal. She sent him the first copy of her hymn "Take my life and let it be consecrated, Lord, to Thee" in manuscript form as soon as it was written. He then helped publicize this hymn through his ministry.

cannot tell when to date my conversion!

It is rather curious how all along He has been keeping me _isolated_. I have hardly read anything about it. I have been to _no_ meeting, nor come in contact with _any_ teacher, except meeting Mr. Smith at Leamington and hearing that one address of yours at Mildmay (July/74). I wonder whether this is that I may not _echo phraseology_? But that in what I say or write, I may express myself more _freshly_ than I should probably do if I had been hearing a _great many_ addresses— it would be so difficult to avoid unconsciously or even consciously reproducing the words and _form_ of ideas which one had been drinking in. For I know He is teaching me the _same_ things which I should have been learning at Brighton and Oxford if I had been able to go. Nevertheless, if He did open the way for me to go, I should not thankfully embrace the opportunity of further help through human channels. I should not have inflicted such a screed on you, but that you expressed a wish to know.

Yours in heartfelt love,

Frances R. Havergal

Part Two: Social Change

"'Behold, I make all things new' was the joyful declaration of woman's great Deliverer. 'He hath sent me to heal the broken-hearted, to preach deliverance to the captives, and recovering of sight to the blind, to set at liberty them that are bruised.' Above all other beings these words must refer to woman, who, without Christ, lies prostrate under society's pitiless and crushing pyramid."

-Francis Willard
Women in the Pulpit (1888), page 51.

Frances Willard (Sept. 28, 1839-Feb. 17, 1898)
(Image in the Public Domain)

Biography

Frances Elizabeth Caroline Willard (Sept. 28, 1839-Feb. 17, 1898) was born in New York, but as an infant, her father moved the family to Oberlin College in Ohio to study for the ministry. Oberlin was known for its holiness roots, but also with strong feelings about the abolition of slavery. It is the oldest college to take students of all races, and to be co-educational as well. In 1846, the family moved to Wisconsin, where they became Methodists. Frances Willard would remain a strongly religious Methodist for the rest of her life.

After a short stint as the first Dean of women at Northwestern University, Willard became involved in the temperance movement. In 1874 she was part of the founding conference of the Woman's Christian Temperance Union. She started as the first Corresponding Secretary and then moved into the publishing branches of the organization before becoming the second president in 1879. With her personal secretary Anna Adams Gordon, she became a major advocate for temperance and built up the W.C.T.U. to one of the largest women's organizations in the world. Ultimately united many of the different national organizations in the World's Woman's Christian Temperance Association were brought together in 1888.

Willard had a much broader view of the temperance movement than many. She saw the equality of men and women as part of the divine laws of God, so that leadership in the family as well as the nation should be shared by both genders. Temperance was seen as a way to protect the family from physical violence and economic destruction. Women's right to vote were seen as a way to further the cause of temperance by creating laws to further protect the family from the liquor traffic by empowering women. Willard's death at 58 years of age kept her from seeing the fulfillment of her goals of prohibition and women's right to vote, but her work was instrumental in the future success of both of these causes.

"BE NOT OVERCOME OF EVIL, BUT OVERCOME EVIL WITH GOOD."

National Woman's Christian Temperance Union.

Headquarters 161 La Salle St.,

CHICAGO.

PRES'T, FRANCES E. WILLARD.
COR. SEC'Y, CAROLINE B. BUELL.
REC. SEC'Y, MARY A. WOODBRIDGE.
ASS'T REC. SEC'Y, L. M. N. STEVENS.
TREAS., ESTHER PUGH.

PRESIDENT'S OFFICE.

ANNA A. GORDON, PRIVATE SECRETARY.
ALICE E. BRIGGS, OFFICE SECRETARY.

Evanston, Ill., Oct 6 1890.

Dearest Hannah:

Here is thy Pall Mall Constitution. It about what one would expect. Guess thee would do better. I would not touch the poor old book again. Thee are too much underwater with current cares. You are I am possib't of Worcels of National Council of Woman's Council which tells

Evanston, Ill.
Oct. 6, 1890

Dearest Hannah:

Here's thy constitution. <u>Pall Mall</u> is about what one would expect. Guess <u>Stead</u> would do better. I <u>cannot</u> touch the poor old book again. Am too much <u>underwater</u> with current cares. You see I am president of World's and National W.C.T.U. and of <u>Woman's Council</u>, which holds

its great meeting in
Pike's Opera House
Washington Street
Spring. Am so
away but the work
blocked out ought
to occupy a full
10 women.

Hear?

It occurs to me that
the leaflets I enclose could
be used in your new
edition. Much left for a
&c. Also some anything from
my annual address that you
can — all these will be
helpful. Take

its great meeting in Pike's Opera House Washington next spring. Am so sorry but the work blocked out ought to _occupy_ and _kill_ 10 women.

Hear?

It occurs to me that the leaflets I enclose could be used in your new edition—White Life for 2 etc.—Also take anything from my Annual address that you like—all these will be helpful. Take

"BE NOT OVERCOME OF EVIL BUT OVERCOME EVIL WITH GOOD."

National Woman's Christian Temperance Union.

Headquarters 161 La Salle St.,

CHICAGO.

PRES'T, FRANCES E. WILLARD.
COR. SEC'Y, CAROLINE B. BUELL.
REC. SEC'Y, MARY A. WOODBRIDGE.
ASS'T REC. SEC'Y, L. M. N. STEVENS.
TREAS., ESTHER PUGH.

PRESIDENT'S OFFICE.

ANNA A. GORDON, PRIVATE SECRETARY.
ALICE E. BRIGGS, OFFICE SECRETARY.

Evanston, Ill.,   1890.

anything three times from "How to win" (Funk & Wagnalls "have it at their London House) & wish the B.W. by a would keep any of my leaflets in both or those of the W.T.P.a that will help. — all right about

anything thee likes from "How to Win"
(Frank Wagnalls have it at their London
House) I <u>wish</u> the B.W.T.A. would keep
any of my leaflets or books or those of the
W.T.P.A. that will <u>help</u>. — All right about

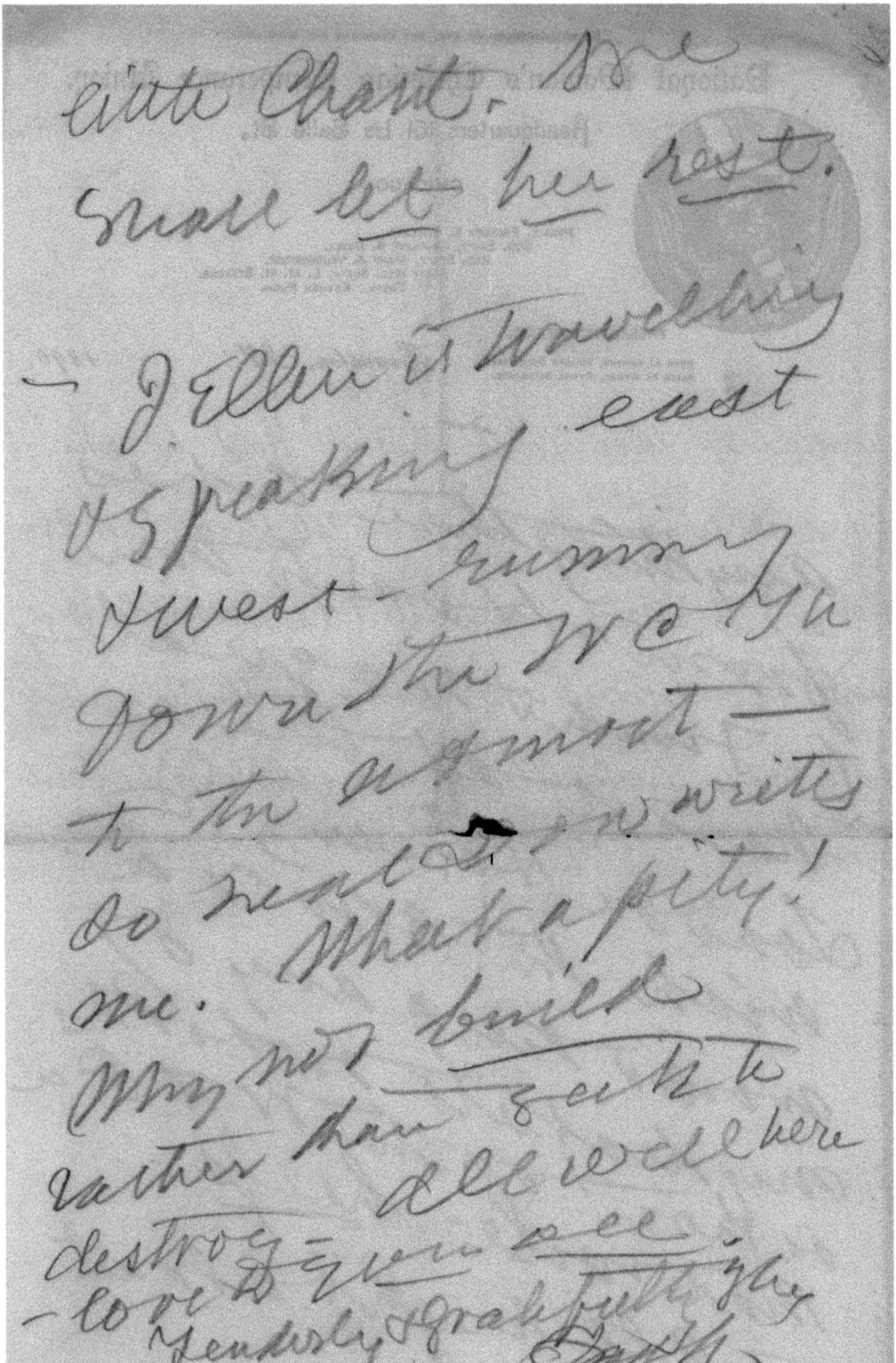

little Chant, we shall let her rest.

J. Ellen is travelling and speaking east and west— running down the W.C.T.U. to the utmost— so Neal Dow writes me. What a pity! Why not build rather than seek to destroy— All well here— love to you all.

Tenderly and gratefully thy

Frances Willard

Notes: This letter was written at the height of Frances Willard's activities. She was president of the National Woman's Christian Temperance Union (W.C.T.U.), the World's Woman's Christian Temperance Association, and president of the National Council of Women of the United States (the "Woman's Council" she mentions) at this time, which are referenced in the letter. Hannah was the Secretary of Evangelism for the W.C.T.U. and was also involved with the British Women's Temperance Association (B.W.T.A.).

The opening of the letter must refer to something that Hannah would like to publish in a British newspaper. The Pall Mall Gazette was a major liberal paper that had helped Josephine Butler uncover the plight of child prostitution under the leadership of W.T. Stead its editor. Stead left the Pall Mall Gazette in 1889 and by 1890 was the editor of the Review of Reviews.

She also refers to two of her books: A White Life for Two (on purity), and How to Win: A Books for Girls. The reference to J. Ellen may refer to Judith Ellen Foster, the W.C.T.U. Superintendent of the legislative department and the first woman allowed to practice law in Iowa. While a strong advocate for temperance, she also fought the idea that any organization could pledge the influence of its members to any other organization, and this might be an area of conflict. Neal Dow was an important politician from Maine who was active in temperance causes. He was the 1880 presidential candidate for the Prohibitionist Party.

Lady Isabella Somerset (Aug. 3, 1851-Mar. 12, 1921)
(Image in the Public Domain)

Biography

Isabella Caroline, Lady Henry Somerset (Aug. 3, 1851-Mar. 12, 1921) was one of the two surviving daughter of the 3rd Earl Somers, and as such she inherited a great deal of wealth. It was considered a good social marriage when she married the second son of the 8th Duke of Beaufort. Lord Henry Somerset in 1872. The couple had one son, but by then Isabella had found out that her husband was homosexual. Given their social standing and the attitude of the day, it was expected that she would turn a blind eye to this behavior. However, Lady Somerset refused to do so and sued for custody of their child. Her suit revealed his sexual orientation and she won custody of her son, but became ostracized by her social circle. Isabella was raised a very religious Anglican and converted to Methodism in the 1880's, so she never divorced Lord Henry, who left England for Italy in 1878.

On the death of her father in 1883 she inherited Eastnor Castle and a large number of other properties. While being socially ostracized by the elite, she turned her attention to social reform in Britain. She became involved in the temperance movement and was known as a very eloquent speaker. In 1890 she was elected president of the British Women's Temperance Union, and after speaking at the World's Women's Christian Temperance Association in 1891 she was elected vice-president of that organization. Besides temperance work, Lady Isabella Somerset also promoted birth control efforts and the emancipation of women. In 1898, at the death of Frances Willard, Lady Somerset was elected president of the World's Woman's Christian Temperance Association, a position she held until 1906.

Eastnor Castle, LEDBURY.

March 2nd 1898.

Dearest Hannah :

I cannot write.   Thy conclusions were all just and true.   I have written a letter to the women that I think thee will approve.   To those who have been true to the principles of love and charity I can never feel grateful enough; and to those who have not, they have had their excuse, only I shall be so glad when we reach the land where motives are as clear as actions.

Now dear, you ask me what the Branches are to do.   Yes, I think they had better propose my re-election even if I cannot do much active work for the present - that is to say, if my re-election is of value.   Dearest Hannah, our loss is irreparably great.   I know not how many years may elapse - perhaps not many, perhaps not even one - before we meet again ; but this I know that eternity is not very far from time, and that I believe her spirit will go with us and abide with us all through the journey that remains, and God does comfort, Hannah, and only God can; only the world is big and grey and lonely, and one feels more truly that Heaven is our home.

Devotedly thine,

Isabel Somerset

Note: This letter is in reference to the death of Frances Willard, who passed away February 18, 1898. Willard was the president of the World's Women's Christian Temperance Association, while Isabella Somerset was the president of the British Women's Temperance Association and became the vice-president of the World's Women's Christian Temperance Association after meeting Willard.

Eastnor Castle, Ledbury
March 2nd, 1898

Dearest Hannah:

I cannot write. Thy conclusions were all just and
true. I have written a letter to the women that I
think thee will approve. To those who have been true
to the principles of love and charity I can never
feel grateful enough; and to those who have not, they
have had their excuse, only I shall be glad when we
reach the land where motives are as clear as actions.

Now dear, you ask me what the branches are
to do. Yes, I think they had better propose my re-
election even if I cannot do much active work for
the present-that is to say, if my re-election is
of value. Dearest Hannah, our loss is irreparably
great. I know not how many years may elapse-perhaps
not many, perhaps not even one-before we meet again;
but this I know that eternity is not very far from
time, and that I believe her spirit will go with
us and abide with us all through the journey that
remains, and God does comfort, Hannah, and only God
can; only the world is big and grey and lonely, and
one feels more truly that Heaven is our home.

Devotedly thine,

Isabel Somerset

Constance Wilde (Holland)(Mrs. Oscar Wilde) (Jan. 2, 1859-Apr. 7, 1898)
(Image in the Public Domain)

Biography

Constance Holland was the changed name of Constance Mary Wilde (Lloyd) (Jan. 2, 1859-Apr. 7, 1898), the wife of Irish playwright Oscar Wilde. The couple had two sons, Cyril and Vyvyan. Constance married Oscar Wilde on May 29, 1884, and shortly thereafter published a book of children's stories. While not an active part of many of the women's movements of the time, Constance was involved in the Dress Reform Movement, which sought to free women from the dangerous constraints of Victorian women's fashions, such as tightly laced corsets that could damage internal organs.

Constance was only 39 when she died after a surgery that is now suspected to have been an attempt to cure a misdiagnosed case of multiple sclerosis. Her life was in large part defined by the scandal that rocked British society in the 1890s. Her husband, a well-known writer, was also homosexual and became involved with Lord Alfred Douglas as his lover. When Lord Alfred Douglas' father, the Marquess of Queensbury publically accused Wilde of his behavior, Wilde sued the Marquess for criminal libel. In the course of the trial the evidence of Wilde's homosexuality emerged and forced him to drop the charges of libel. Wilde was then arrested and charged for gross indecency with men and sentenced for two years hard labor.

In terms of women's issues of the times, Constance's situation represents the lack of rights many women had under the marriage and divorce laws of the Victorian era. When Constance married Oscar Wilde, she came into the marriage with an annual allowance of £250 (about $32,000 at today's rates). Until 1870, married women were considered to legally be one person with their husband. All of their property came to their husband, except real estate, but they could not make any legal decisions about that real estate without the husband's consent. Any income a woman earned or legal copyright for works she produced belonged to her husband. Even at death, a woman's husband could pass her property on in his will to someone else.

The Married Women's Property Act of 1870 did allow some changes, so that women could keep their own earnings and the property they might have inherited. They also were considered legally responsible for the care of children along with their husbands. However the act was not retroactive, so it did not help women married at the time. Additional changes in 1882, 1884, and 1893 opened the way for British women to be seen as legally and financially separate from their husbands and thus legally and financially equal. This was a huge step forward in terms of women's equality.

In the letter to Hannah Whitall Smith, it is clear that Constance has legal rights to restore some of her income to her children, but the social scandal of divorce still kept her legally married to Oscar Wilde for the remainder of her life. The right to divorce still carried with it major stigma for many women in this time period, even when the fault of the divorce was clearly on the behavior of the husband. As such, Constance Holland's letter reveals some of the difficulties women faced in a society where their rights were limited and often controlled by their husbands.

From Mrs. Wilde
who has changed her name
to Holland

Bevaix
Canton Neuchâtel
Oct. 15. 1895

Return to H.W.S.

My dear Mrs. Pearsall Smith,

Thank you very much
indeed for your kind letter
with your report of Lady Mount
Temple who, dear thing, has
written me a most loving
little letter this morning.
She is a very wonderful, &
I hope the business that called
you there was not tiresome for
her.

I have changed my name
but I am not taking any
legal proceedings. My poor
misguided husband, who is

Bevaix

Canton Neuchatel

Oct. 15. 1895

My dear Mrs. Pearsall Smith,

Thank you very much indeed for your kind letter with your report of Lady Mount Temple, who dear thing, has written me a most loving little letter this morning. She is very wonderful and I hope the business that called you then was not tiresome for her.

I have changed my name but I am not taking any legal proceeding. My poor misguided husband; who is

weak, rather than wicked repents
most bitterly all his past madness
and I cannot ~~refuse to him~~ the
forgiveness that he has asked. So
I have withdrawn from the
Divorce proceedings that I was
at one time tempted to institute
against him, or rather that I
was ~~tempted~~ worried to institute for the
sake of my boys. But the
necessity for that is obviated by
the ~~the~~ Bankruptcy proceedings in
which I am claiming through my
Trustees the life = interest of my
money which does at present
belong to my husband, and which

weak rather than wicked regrets most bitterly all his past madness and I cannot refuse to him the forgiveness that he has asked. So I have withdrawn from the divorce proceedings that I was at one time tempted to institute against him, or rather that I was worried to institute for the sake of my boys. But the necessity for that is obviated by the Bankruptcy proceedings in which I am claiming through my Trustees the life interest of my money which does at present belong to my husband and which

will then go straight to the children
after my death.

I can only trust that I have
been guided right, and I have
indeed sought Divine Wisdom,
but things are so complicated
that it is difficult to tell whether
one has been guided right.

I am sure tho that you will
agree with me that where there
is repentance, it is not the place
of the wife to be the Avenger. Just
think what he has lost! Practically
all that made life bearable to him.
I hear from the prison chaplain
& from others who have an opportunity
of judging that he is very heart-

will then go straight to the children after my death.

I can only trust that I have been guided right. and I have indeed sought Divine wisdom. but things are so complicated that it is difficult to tell whether one has been guided right.

I am sure though that you will agree with me that where there is repentance. it is not the place of the wife to be the Avenger. Just think what he has lost! Practically all that made life bearable to him. I hear from the prison chaplain and from others who have an opportunity of judging that he is very heart

= broken and most especially so with
regard to the trouble that he has
brought on my self and the boys.
This address will find me for some
time & a letter addressed to

C/o Miss Boswell
12 Holbein House, S. W.
will always be forwarded.

Aff⁻ᵗᵉˡʸ yours

Constance Holland

broken and most especially so with regard to the trouble that he has brought on myself and the boys. This address will find me for some time and a letter addressed to

c/o Miss Boxwell
12 Holbein House, S.W.

will always be forwarded.

Affectionately yours,

Constance Holland

Mary Clement Leavitt (1830-1912)
(Image in the Public Domain)

Biography

Mary Greenleaf Clement Leavitt (Sept. 22, 1830- Feb. 5, 1912) was born in New Hampshire, the daughter of a Baptist minister. She became a schoolteacher in the Boston area and was briefly married for a short time to Thomas H. Leavitt and had three daughters before being divorced. Through her association with Dwight Moody, she met Frances Willard in 1873 and organized the first Women's Christian Temperance Union chapter in Boston. In 1874 she gave up teaching to travel throughout New England and promote temperance and women's suffrage for the W.C.T.U. She was so successful in this work that she was sent to California, Oregon, and Washington in 1883 to promote the temperance work of the W.C.T.U.

Frances Willard finally decided to use her talents globally, naming Leavitt the "Superintendent of Reconnaissance for World's WCTU." In 1884, Leavitt left the U.S. at 54 years old to become the first global missionary of the Women's Christian Temperance Union. She bought her own ticket to Hawaii and left with $35 to travel the world. After Hawaii, Leavitt went to Australia where she met considerable success. From there she travelled almost non-stop and visited New Zealand, Tasmania, Japan, China, Siam, Singapore and the Malay Peninsula, Burma, India, Ceylon, Mauritius, Madagascar, Natal, Orange Free State, Great Britain, Congo, Sierra Leon, Spain, France, Norway, Sweden, Finland, Denmark, Germany, Italy, Greece, Egypt, Syria, and Turkey. She always paid for her travel from her own money or funds raised in the place she was currently visiting, saving official funds to help fund other global missionaries of the temperance movement.

By the halfway point of her travels, the W.C.T.U. reported she had founded 86 branches of the W.C.T.U. around the globe, travelled over 100,000 miles through 43 countries and held over 1,600 meetings in 47 different languages! Leavitt questioned British rule in India and influenced Pandita Ramabai along with thousands of other women around the world. She became an Honorary Life President of the W.C.T.U., before ultimately withdrawing from the group. She considered her most important work, not the promotion of temperance, but the development of connections and fellowship among women in remote parts of the world.

answered

Sydney, Australia
Th. Aug 13, 1885.

Dear Mrs. Smith,

I see by a recent American paper that you are by this time in England, I hope on a Wider field mission. If so please write to me its purport. In any case I trust if there is an opportunity to prepare the way for my coming, you will speak the word that will help. I shall be much pleased if you can send me a name or two of people with whom I can correspond.

I met a Rev. Mr. Hill, Anglican missionary in Auckland, an earnest servant of the Lord, and my chief helper there, who owes, he says, what he is spiritually to you, under the Lord. I find your

Sydney, Australia
Thurs. Aug. 13, 1885

Dear Mrs. Smith,

I see by a recent American paper that you are by this time in England. I hope on a W.C.T.U. mission. If so please write me its prospects. In any case, I trust if there is an opportunity to prepare the way for my coming you will speak the word that will help. I shall be much pleased if you can send me a name or two of people with whom I can correspond.

I met a Rev. Mr. Hill, Anglican missionary in Auckland, an excellent servant of the Lord, and my chief helper there, who owes, he says what he is spiritually to you, under the Lord. I find your

writings in many households
and have met several persons
who attended your meetings in
England.

May you be blessed of the
Lord during your absence from
home, whether it be for rest
or for work.

Please direct a word of
reply to Melbourne, Australia,
C/o Rev. Mr. Budlong, Pastor
of Cairns Memorial Church

With love,
Very truly,
Mary Clement Leavitt.

writings in many households and have met several persons who attended your meetings in England.

May you be blessed of the Lord during your absence from home, whether it is for rest or for work.

Please direct a word of reply to Melbourne, Australia, c/o Rev. Mr. Buchannan Pastor of Cairns Memorial Church.

With love,

Very truly,

Mary Clement Leavitt

Part Three: Political Activism

"I cannot tell you how rejoiced I have been in listening to the papers which have been read here to see the liberality of spirit, to see the growing feeling of recognition of everybody who has inside what the Quakers used to call 'the light that lighteth every man that cometh into the world,' and consequently, the old Quaker preacher used to say, 'every woman.' He always had to add that. I have heard that preached in a singsong tone thousands of times, and that was the difference between the Quakers and other religious sects. The Quakers always believed 'consequently woman.' Whatever right or duty or privilege was spoken of as having been obtained for man was 'consequently for woman.'"

- Susan B. Anthony

"The Moral Leadership of the Religious Press" speech given May 27, 1893

Susan B. Anthony (Feb. 15, 1820–Mar. 13, 1906)
(Image in the Public Domain)

Biography

Susan Brownell Anthony (Feb. 15, 1820-Mar. 13, 1906) was born into a Quaker family, and with her friend and co-worker, Elizabeth Cady Stanton, became a major force for social reform in the United States. Her early Quaker background in New York brought her into the movements for the abolition of slavery, temperance, and women's rights. In 1863, they founded the Women's Loyal National League, which advocated the abolition of slavery, followed by a paper for women's rights called *The Revolution* and the National Woman Suffrage Association in the late 1860s.

In 1872, Anthony was arrested for illegally voting and went to trial, where she dramatically and passionately defended the right of women to be treated as equal citizens in one of the most famous speeches ever given for women's rights. (For an account of the trial see: http://ecssba.rutgers.edu/docs/sbatrial.html) She refused to pay the fine and the government refused to take the issue further. In 1878, along with Elizabeth Cady Stanton, Susan B. Anthony advanced an amendment giving women the right to vote. It would ultimately become the Nineteenth Amendment of the U.S. Constitution. In 1979 her image became the first image of an American woman on a U.S. coin.

Anthony never married, in part because of the legal subjugation she felt that entailed. Had she married she would have been unable to sign contracts on her own behalf. Laws gave husbands absolute control over the family and its finances. This was one reason the Temperance Movement was seen as a woman's issue. Men who abused alcohol could completely destroy their families with no legal recourse. Even if a husband was abusive, if a woman was able to gain a very rare divorce, usually the husband ended up with custody of any children. She is quoted as saying in 1877, "If women will not accept marriage with subjugation, nor men proffer it without, there is, there can be, no alternative. The woman who will not be ruled must live without marriage."

Fortieth Anniversary of the Woman Suffrage Movement.

International Council of Women

ASSEMBLED BY THE

National Woman Suffrage Association

of the United States,

To be held at Washington, D. C., March 25 to April 1, 1888, inclusive.

COMMITTEE OF ARRANGEMENTS:

ELIZABETH CADY STANTON, PRESIDENT.	RACHEL G. FOSTER, COR. SEC.,
SUSAN B. ANTHONY, ROCHESTER, N. Y.,	748 N. 19TH ST., PHILADELPHIA.
MATILDA JOSLYN GAGE, FAYETTEVILLE, N. Y.,	ELLEN H. SHELDON, REC. SEC.
VICE-PRESIDENTS AT LARGE.	Q. M. GENERAL'S OFFICE, WASHINGTON, D. C.
MAY WRIGHT SEWALL, CHAIRMAN EX. COM.,	JANE H. SPOFFORD, TREASURER,
343 N. PENNSYLVANIA ST., INDIANAPOLIS, IND.	RIGGS HOUSE, WASHINGTON, D. C.

Riggs House Washington D. C. Jan. 19, 1888

My Dear Mrs Smith

I received your note when in Phila. a week ago — and answered it to the address you gave me — but I fear you did not get it — So write to-night to make sure there is no failure — We devote the 2d eve'g — Tuesday — to Temperance — Miss Willard will speak for the National W. C. T. U. and we want you or whoever you prefer — to speak 10 or 15 minutes for the World's Temp. Union — — will you

Riggs House, Washington, D.C. Jan. 19, 1888

My Dear Mrs. Smith

I received your note when in Philadelphia
A week ago and answered it to the address
you gave me — but I fear you did not get it — so
write tonight to make sure there shall be no
failure — We devote the 2nd evening — Tuesday
to Temperance — Miss Willard will speak for
the National W.C.T.U. and we want you or
whoever you prefer — to speak 10 or 15 minutes
for the World's Temperance Union — Will you

write me here – or to Miss Foster –
748 – North 19th st – Phila – Who is to be
your delegate – at earliest moment –
We are trying hard to get our delegates
& speakers settled into a program – which
is no small matter for an eight
days – sixteen session – Council!

I hear you are to be in
Wash. with Miss Willard the
week previous to the Council –
I am glad of it – Washington
ought to be stormed with
women demanding to be
heard every winter – The
Powers that be" – not ordained
of God" – must not be obeyed –
At least without constant protest!

So good night with love –

Susan B. Anthony

write me here— or to Miss Foster—748 North 17th St— Philadelphia—who is to be your delegate—at earliest moment—We are trying hard to get our delegates and speakers settled into a program—which is no small matter for an eight days—sixteen session—Council!

I hear you are to be in Washington with Miss Willard the week previous to the Council—I am glad of it—Washington ought to be _stormed_ with women demanding to be heard every winter—"The Powers that be" —_not_ "ordained of God" —must not be obeyed—at least without constant protest!

So good night with love.

Susan B. Anthony

Clara Barton (Dec. 25, 1821–Apr. 12, 1912)
(Image in the Public Domain)

Biography

Clarissa "Clara" Harlowe Barton (Dec. 25, 1821-Apr. 12, 1912) became involved in nursing when she was 10 years old, as she took care of her brother who had suffered a fall from a barn roof. She was naturally very shy and timid and did not make friends easily, often succumbing to bouts of depression. Her parents convinced her to become a schoolteacher, and this helped her a great deal with her self-confidence. She worked her way up to running a large successful school in 1852, only to be replaced by a male principal, since such a role was seen as unfitting for a woman.

In 1855 she took a job at the U.S. Patent Office in Washington D.C. as a clerk, one of the first women to work in such a position with a salary equal to the male clerks. The abuse and political opposition to her role was so great her position was ultimately reduced to that of "copyist" and she was fired.

On April 19, 1861 some of the first wounded of the Civil War were brought to Washington, and they came from the 6th Massachusetts Militia, including young men from Clara's hometown and even former students. She became involved in collecting supplies, nursing the wounded, and writing letters for the soldiers she cared for. She was soon appointed to work on the front lines caring for the Union wounded, becoming known as the "Angel of the Battlefield." After the war she ran the Office of Missing Soldiers, helping loved ones find and bury their loved ones who were in unmarked graves.

After the war, Barton became associated with Susan B. Anthony and the work of women's suffrage. She also travelled to Switzerland, where she learned of the work of the Red Cross, and she would ultimately become the leader of the American Red Cross. She worked in the Franco-Prussian War and was decorated with the Golden Cross of Baden and the Prussian Iron Cross for her nursing work. She was also on the front lines with the American Red Cross at the Johnstown Flood in 1889 and the Galveston Hurricane in 1900. Some of her final work was a response to the massacre and famine in Armenia of Armenian Christians by the Turks. Even up until her death at 90 years old, Clara Barton, who was not particularly religious, identified herself as a Universalist.

From the leader of
the "Red Cross" movement

Please return to H.W.S.

VICTORIA STREET,

LONDON, S.W.

_____ 189__

Dear Mrs. Smith —

We are very desirous of meeting the committee† and *can* extend our stay until Wednesday morning 11 o'clock, when it is arranged for us to leave

We shall be most happy to meet the committee on Tuesday Evening

We shall be here at after 4 o'clock tomorrow afternoon

† Duke of Westminster (sen.)

Victoria Street, London, S.W.

189 —

Dear Mrs. Smith —

We are very desirous of meeting the committee (Duke of Westminster Com.) and can extend our stay until Wednesday morning 11 o'clock when it is arranged for us to leave. We shall be most happy to meet the committee on Tuesday evening.

We shall be home at or after 4 o'clock tomorrow afternoon

and would be most
happy to meet Mr. and
Mrs. Harris at that
time, or rather at any
time after that knew that
it is their preference to
call. Thanking you for
your kindness I am.
Most cordially

Clara Barton
You will kindly inform us where
and at what hour we can meet the
committee. on Tuesday Evening
oblige.

and would be most happy to meet Mr.
and Mrs. Harris at that time, or
rather at any time after that hour
that it is their preference to call.

Thanking you for your kindness I am,

Most cordially,
Clara Barton

You will kindly inform us where and at
what hour we can meet the committee on
Tuesday evening.

Note: Mr. and Mrs. Harris may refer to James Rendel Harris (1852-1941) and his wife Helen Balkwill Harris, who were Quakers. They were involved in relief and mission work in Turkish Armenia in the 1890's dealing with massacres of the Armenians at that time. Clara Barton was also involved in relief work in Asia Minor under the Red Cross at this same time. Hugh Grosvenor, the First Duke of Westminster (1825-1899) was involved in a number of charities and Helen Harris mentions a relief centre receiving help from the "Duke of Westminster's Fund" in one of her published letters about the work in Armenia. The Duke had also previous been head of the Queen's Jubilee Nursing Fund, and through association had come to know Florence Nightingale. In 1896, when she was 75, Clara Barton led a contingent of Red Cross workers to the Ottoman Empire because of famine and the Armenian massacres by the Turks. It is not clear what was Hannah's involvement with the Duke of Westminster Committee.

Martha Carey Thomas (Jan. 2, 1857-Dec. 2, 1935)
(Image in the Public Domain)

Biography

Martha Carey Thomas (Jan. 2, 1857-Dec. 2, 1935) was a graduate of Cornell University and went on to earn a Ph.D. in Linguistics from the University of Zurich in 1882. She was the first woman and first foreigner to receive a doctorate from the university. She also attended classes at the University of Leipzig and the Sorbonne in Paris. She returned to the United States to be the dean of Bryn Mawr College. In 1894 she became the second president of Bryn Mawr College, a position she held until 1922.

In 1908, Carey Thomas became the first president of the National College Women's Equal Suffrage League, in addition to being active in the National American Woman Suffrage Association. After women won the right to vote, she became a major advocate for the National Woman's Party and one of the first to push for an equal rights amendment to the U.S. Constitution.

Carey Thomas was also instrumental in creating the Bryn Mawr Summer School for Women Workers in Industry (1921-1938), which was an experimental program to help provide academic education to young women, who were mostly factory workers with very little education. Many of these women went on to take leading positions in trade unions and in their local communities, very much in line with the legacy of Hannah Whitall Smith.

While there is no letter in the collection from Martha Carey Thomas, her life and activities give us a place to refer to the influence Robert Pearsall Smith and Hannah Whitall Smith had within their own family circle. Married on November 5, 1851, the couple had seven children, but only three lived to become adults. Their only son, Logan Pearsall Smith, was educated in Harvard and Oxford and became a writer and critic with a special interest in 17th century divines.

Hannah and Robert's daughter, Mary, was married twice. First she married an Irish barrister, Benjamin Conn "Frank" Costelloe. They had two daughters: Ray Strachey and Karin Stephen. Mary later divorced Costelloe and married art historian, Bernard Berenson, who was an authority on Renaissance art. Mary's eldest daughter, Rachel Pearsall Costelloe married Oliver Strachey in 1911. He was the son of Jane Maria Strachey, a well-known British suffragette who was one of the leaders of the Mud March of 1907. Ray Strachey, herself would become a major part of the British suffrage movement and wrote a book called *The Cause* in 1928. After women received the right to vote she ran for political office a number of times without success. Catherine Elizabeth Costelloe married Adrian Stephen, the brother of Virginia Woolf, in 1914. Known as Karin, she became a psychoanalyst and psychologist, but the couple continued the family tradition of social activism by being conscientious objectors during World War I.

Hannah and Robert's second daughter, Alyssa Pearsall Smith was the first wife of the British philosopher and Nobel laureate, Bertrand Russell, known for his political activism and writing. Alys separated from Russell in 1911, and they divorced in 1921. She worked with Italian refugees during World War II, and established a School for Mothers in London, in an effort to reduce infant mortality.

Martha Carey Thomas, was a niece of Hannah Whitall Smith, the daughter of her sister Mary Whitall Thomas. Known as Carey Thomas, she was greatly influenced by the feminism of her mother and her aunt. Carey was especially close to Hannah's son Frank, who died in 1872. Her later accomplishments, and well as those of Hannah's own daughters reflect on how Hannah's social activism and feminist ideals influenced women around her through her personal connections as well as her correspondence.

Biography

Annie Leigh Browne (Mar. 14, 1851-Mar. 8, 1936)

(No Image Available)

Anne Leigh Browne (Mar. 14, 1851-Mar. 8, 1936) was born into a well-off family in the United Kingdom that provided her with tutors and governesses and even sent her to Queens College on Harley Street for a year. The same year she was in college she was invited to what many consider the first women's suffrage meeting with Mary Carpenter at the home of John Beddoe and his wife. While Browne was committed to the suffragist movement, her real passion was for education and bringing women into public office.

In 1880 she, along with Mary Stewart Kilgour worked hard as advocates for women's education and their work led to the opening of College Hall in 1882. Much of this was made possible with Browne's financing of the endeavor. In 1888, Browne once against used her funds to join eleven other women in forming the "Society for Promoting the Return of Women as County Councilors", which became the "Women's Local Government Society" in 1893. The aim was to elect women to local government positions, especially in areas where they were not distinctly forbidden to run. Two women were elected to the London County Council because of the unclear wording of the Local Government Act 1888, but a court case later disqualified the women. In 1894 new legislation was passed that did allow married women to hold some offices such as on school boards.

Browne remained a major part of the suffrage movement, serving on the executive committee of the Union of Practical Suffragists, and being an active member of the Central Society for Women's Suffrage and the London Society for Women's Suffrage. She took part in the famous "Mud March" of February 7, 1907, the first mass procession of British suffragists, when 3,000 women marched in the muddy streets of London. This procession was part of the organizing genius of Philippa Strachey, the sister of Oliver Strachey, who married Hannah Whitall Smith's granddaughter, Ray Costelloe.

The Society for Promoting the Return of Women to
all Local Governing Bodies.

President—THE COUNTESS OF ABERDEEN.

Hon. Sec.—Miss Browne, 58, Porchester Terrace, W.
Hon. Treasurer—Miss M. S. Kilgour, 46, Porchester Road, W.

Feb. 13. 94

Dear Mrs Pearsall Smith,

Could you spare half
an hour for me to call upon
you to speak about a resolution
we are going to ask you to
move on the 16th inst. The
draft cannot be quite
fixed until the last on
account of the changes made

Feb. 13. 1894

Dear Mrs. Pearsall Smith.

Could you spare half an hour for me to
call upon you to speak about a resolution
we are going to ask you to move on the 16th
inst. The draft cannot be quick—fixed until
the last on account of the changes made

by the action of the
House of Lords in
the Local Gov^t Bill,
but if you could let me
call upon you on
Thursday next, 15th,
after 2 p.m., or if the
afternoon be not convenient
at 11 a.m. I enclose
a card of reminder for
the meeting.

Yours truly

Annie Leigh Browne

pp. D. Unh.

by the action of the House of Lords in the Local Govt. Bill, but if you could let me call upon you on Thursday next, 15th, after 2 PM, or if the afternoon cannot be convenient at 11 AM. I enclose a card of reminder for the meeting.

Yours truly,

Anne Leigh Browne

Part Four: Cultural Transformation

After giving her first speech on Women's Suffrage…

"I am thoroughly roused on the subject for I have had so many cases of grievous oppression of men over their wives lately that my blood boils with indignation. And before thee is married I want to have thy position as the equal of thy husband settled on a legal basis. The moment one looks into the subject at all it seems utterly incomprehensible how we women could have endured it as patiently as we have. Literally and truly up to within a few years women have been simple slaves. And some women say they like it! Ugh! It is one of the worst vices of slavery that its victims are contented with their lot."

Letter from Hannah Whitall Smith to her daughter Mary (1882) Recorded on page 55 of Barbara Strachy's *Remarkable Relations: The Story of the Pearsall Smith Women* (1980).

Josephine E. Butler (Apr. 13, 1828-Dec. 30, 1906)
(Image in the Public Domain)

Biography

Josephine Elizabeth Butler (Apr. 13, 1828-Dec. 30, 1906) was born into a privileged family, whose father believed that girls as well as boys should be educated in politics and social issues. In her teen years she experienced a religious crisis that made her critical of the Anglican Church, but prompted a deep individual Christian spiritually apart from the organized church. In 1850 she married George Butler, a Fellow at Exeter College in Oxford. Scholarly males who expressed that moral failures in women were worse than in men offended her in conversations in her husband's social circles. It came to their attention of a young unmarried woman in Newgate prison whom a university don had seduced and who in despair had killed her newborn baby. Deeply affected by the story, the Butlers arranged to have the woman live in their house for the remaineder of her sentence.

After the accidental death of one of her children, Josephine decided to become more involved in helping the poor of society. She began to visit the workhouse in Liverpool, where they had recently moved, and she spoke and prayed with many of the women there. She created several homes for women dying in the terminal stages of venereal disease after she ran out of space for them in her own home. At the same time, she became involved in the rights of women to vote and to allow married women to own their own property instead of it automatically becoming their husband's possession.

In 1869, Josephine became aware of the Contagious Disease Acts of 1864, 1866, and 1869, which allowed police to imprison women in special hospitals if they considered them prostitutes. No evidence was needed except the officer's word and the women were forcibly given genital examinations for venereal disease. Women who fought against the examinations would be imprisoned with hard labor. Many lower class women had their reputations destroyed as a result of these acts and many had to turn to prostitution as their only alternative for work after being publically declared to be prostitutes by the officers. There were no penalties for men for seeking prostitutes. Finally in 1886 the acts were formally repealed due to Butler's efforts.

In her investigations into the issue of prostitution and the Contagious Disease Acts, she found cases of prostitutes as young as 12, and further evidence of a slave trade in young girls from England to the European continent for prostitution. She became involved in publicizing this reality and was prominent in exposing sex trade offences in Belgium, Britain, and India as well. She opposed so-called purity societies that attempted to force people to be moral, which she felt was impossible. She wrote over 90 books and pamphlets, and was an essential part in the passing of laws which raised the age of sexual consent from 13 to 16 years of age, made it a crime to abduct a girl under 18 for sexual purposes, and repealed the Contagious Diseases Acts.

As a devout Anglican, Butler was honored by being celebrated in the Church of England with a Lesser Festival on the 30th of May. She saw her work and her feminism as an expression of her Christian faith, and it has been reported that her favorite phrase was, "God and one woman make a majority."

Florence . Dec 10 . 93

My dear Friend Comments on Cath'n & Vatican Get

  I am leaving here for
Rome , where my address
will be Hotel Italie , and I
feel a desire just to tell you
how I have fared so far.
I have been here, about
a fortnight , and have
seen a good many people
of the right sort : I see there
is a good field in Tuscany,
The Tuscans are open minded
& generous , & more moral
than the Southern Italians.
I believe a spark is already
lighted , for our Purity cause,
and of that spark there
may come some purifying
fire , if fanned by the

Florence
Dec. 10 . 1893

My dear friend,

I am leaving here for Rome, where
my address will be Hotel Italie, and I
feel a desire just to tell you how I have
fared so far. I have been in Italy about
a fortnight, and have seen a good many
people of the right sort. I see there is a
good field in Tuscany. The Tuscans are open
minded and generous, and more moral
than the Southern Italians. I believe a
spark is already lighted, for our purity
cause, and of that spark there may come
some purifying fire, if it is fanned by the

breath of God. It has been
a very interesting and instructive
time to me. I have made
myself acquainted with the
present state of Italian
politics, wh is confused &
complex. Our former ally
Crispi seems likely to be
prime minister, if he can
succeed in forming a Cabinet.
There are some very noble
ladies here — noble by birth
& in character, catholics
but liberal, who will lend
their drawingrooms for
meetings when — if it please
God — I return this way
from Southern Italy.
    I hear an exceedingly bad
account of the morals of

breath of God. It has been a very interesting and instructive time to me. I have made myself acquainted with the present state of Italian politics, which is confused and complex. Our former ally Crispi seems likely to be Prime Minister, if he can succeed in forming a cabinet. There are some very noble ladies here— noble by birth and in character, Catholics but liberal, who will lend their drawing rooms for meetings when—if it please God— I return this way from Southern Italy.

I hear an exceeding bad account of the _morals_ of

the Vatican. It is said
(but in whispers) "It is nothing
but a house of prostitution"
& this, it was imagined would
be so discouraging perhaps to
me that I would not approach
it. I was lying on my bed
resting, after some friends
(Italians) had spoken to me
of the corruption of the high
Ecclesiastics, & the thought
came to me, "if ~~it is~~ the Vatican
is a house of prostitution,
how suitable it is that I
should enter it, if God leads
me there! for was I not
called to work for and
among prostitutes? Perhaps
the hearts of prostitute Cardinals
may ~~not~~ be altogether given
up to sin." ~~Yet~~ I am sure
God has some, however, who

the Vatican. It is said (but in whispers)
"It is nothing but a house of prostitution,"
and this, it was imagined would be so
discouraging perhaps to me that I would
not approach it. I was lying on my bed
resting, after some friends (Italians) had
spoken to me of the corruption of the high
ecclesiastics, and the thought came to me,
"if the Vatican is a house of prostitution,
how suitable it is that I should enter
it, if God leads me there! For was I not
called to work for and among prostitutes?
Perhaps the hearts of prostitute Cardinals
may yet not be altogether given up to sin."
I am sure God has some however who

are just & good men among
the Roman clergy. I make
no special effort in any one
direction, but try to bring my message
to "all sorts and conditions
of men."

Please consider what I have
said as confidential; but
send my letter, if it is worth,
to Miss Willard and Lady Henry,
just to let them know that God is
giving me openings. I have
been reading Lady Henry's magnificent speech at Coventgarden
Theatre (was it?) and somebody
writes me that Miss Willard was
there & is so much better. I do
praise God for that. So many
have prayed for her.
I am alone - but possibly my
sister Mrs Meuricoffre may join
me in Rome.
Give my kindest regards to your
daughter & to Mr Pearsall Smith
& believe me yours affect'y
Josephine E Butler

are just and good men among the Roman clergy. I make no special effort in any one direction, but try to bring my message to " all sorts and conditions of men. "

Please consider what I have said as confidential; but send my letter, if it is worthy to Miss Willard and Lady Henry, just to let them know that God is giving me openings. I have been reading Lady Henry's magnificent speech at Covent Garden Theatre (was it?) and somebody writes me that Miss Willard was there and is so much better. I do praise God for that. So many have prayed for her. I am alone—but possibly my sister Mrs. Meuricoffre may join me in Rome. Give my kindest regards to your daughter and Mr. Pearsall Smith and believe me yours affectionately.

Josephine E. Butler

Frances Power Cobbe (Dec. 4, 1822–Apr. 5, 1904)
(Image in the Public Domain)

Biography

Frances Power Cobbe (Dec. 4, 1822-Apr. 5, 1904) was born in Ireland to a large and important family. She grew up as the only daughter of five children and was educated to be a socially acceptable young lady. However, she had a keen mind and disliked social events, preferring to study on her own and enjoy the natural world around her. While her family was quite religious, she ended up rejecting the Christian faith for her own form of belief as an agnostic. But despite this rejection of Christianity, she later wrote, "By far the most important result of the Individualism of the Evangelical System has been the recognition of the spiritual equality of women" (Mitchell 2004:57). In 1855 she published *The Theory of Intuitive Morals*, arguing her own view of Kant's moral imperative.

After her father's death, Cobbe travelled to the Middle East and became a correspondent for the *London Daily News* in Italy. She would go on to a successful journalistic career writing for social progress in a number of papers. Cobbe also continued with her interest in religious thought by becoming a Theist and writing *Broken Lights: an Inquiry into the Present Condition and Future Prospects of Religious Faith* (1864) and *Dawning Lights: an Inquiry Concerning the Secular Results of the New Reformation* (1867).

Cobbe took up the cause of suffrage for women and a concern for abused women. Her article, "Truth on Wife Torture" (1878) became the basis for a law allowing for women to legally separate from husbands convicted of assaulting them. She would develop a greater awareness of ethics as they relate to animals as well as humans, and this led to her forming the Society for the Protection of Animals Liable to Vivisection (SPALV) in 1875 and in 1898 the British Union for the Abolition of Vivisection (BUAV). She became most well known for her anti-vivisection work, but continued writing. Her books include: *On the Pursuits of Women* (1863), *Cities of the Past* (1864), *Criminals, Idiots, Women and Minors* (1869), *Darwinism in Morals* (1871), and *Scientific Spirit of the Age* (1888).

Cobbe is also known for her relationship with Mary Lloyd, an artist who shared her concerns. Their open lesbian relationship lasted from 1864 until Mary's death in 1896. While they seem far apart in terms of theology, Cobbe sought Hannah Whitall Smith's advice to find a leader in the U.S. to help integrate her anti-vivisection views with the larger audience of the Women's Christian Temperance Union. With Smith's support, Frances Willard added mercy to animals as part of the WCTU's work reaching hundreds of thousands of women in America with the anti-vivisection message (Mitchell 2004:327).

answered
Jan. 13. 1889
Within a packet of papers.

Hengwrt,
Dolgelley,
N. Wales.

Jan. 4ᵗʰ

Dear Mrs. Pearsall Smith, —

I am going to claim the acquaintance ~~~ which you so kindly made by letter a couple of years ago, & which I had the pleasure of ratifying by our being hand-shaking at the Meeting in Westminster Palace Hotel, last summer.

I know how sincerely you

Hengwert
Dolgelley
N. Wales

Jan. 9th (note: Answered Jan. 13. 1889)

Dear Mrs. Pearsall Smith.

I am going to claim the acquaintance which you so kindly made by letter a couple of years ago. and which I had the pleasure of ratifying by our brief handshaking at the meeting in Westminster Palace Hotel. last summer.

I know how sincerely you

sympathize with the efforts of
our Victoria St Society to put an
end to Scientific cruelty; I
have therefore no fear in
addressing you concerning the
extension of our work in
America. I hear from many
sources there, so much of your
Great influence among the
most serious-minded people,
from whom our real helps

sympathize with the efforts of our Victoria
St. Society to put an end to scientific
cruelty, and I have therefore no fear in
addressing you concerning the latest here
of our work in America. I hear from
many sources there, so much of your
great influence among the most serious
minded people (from whom our real help

[... ...] that I am most anxious to invoke it in [...], especially (for the reasons I [shall] explain) at this moment.

As you are no doubt aware there exists in Philadelphia an excellent Anti Vivisection Society, founded several years ago by Mrs Richard P. White (a Roman Catholic) & Miss Adèle Biddle. Commenced on the principle of [...] Restriction, this Society [...]

Your affectionate friend [...]

of course must come). Though I am most
anxious to invoke it in aiding us, especially
(per the reasons I shall explain) <u>at this
moment</u>.

As you are no doubt aware there exists in
Philadelphia an excellent Anti—Vivisection
Society, founded several years ago by Wm.
Richard. P. White (a Roman Catholic)
and Miss Adele Biddle. Commenced on
the principles of seeking restitution, this
society last year, with great good sense

adopted our programme of total abolition. This is now fairly on the way, & I think my have a great future of good work before it. It is a larger organization, however, by far, which I have hoped my be brought to ally itself with the same object; — Mrs Willard's marvelous "Christian Women's Temperance Union", of which, of course you know infinitely more than I do & you will need no party explanation when I tell my dear Mrs Willard (with whom adopted our programme of total abolition. It is now fairly on the way and I trust may have a real future of good work before it. W.T.'s a larger organization, however, by far, which I am hopeful may be brought to ally itself with the same object; Miss Willard's marvelous "Christian Women's Temperance Union," of which, of course you know infinitely more than I do. You will need no further explanation when I tell you this dear Miss Willard, (with whom

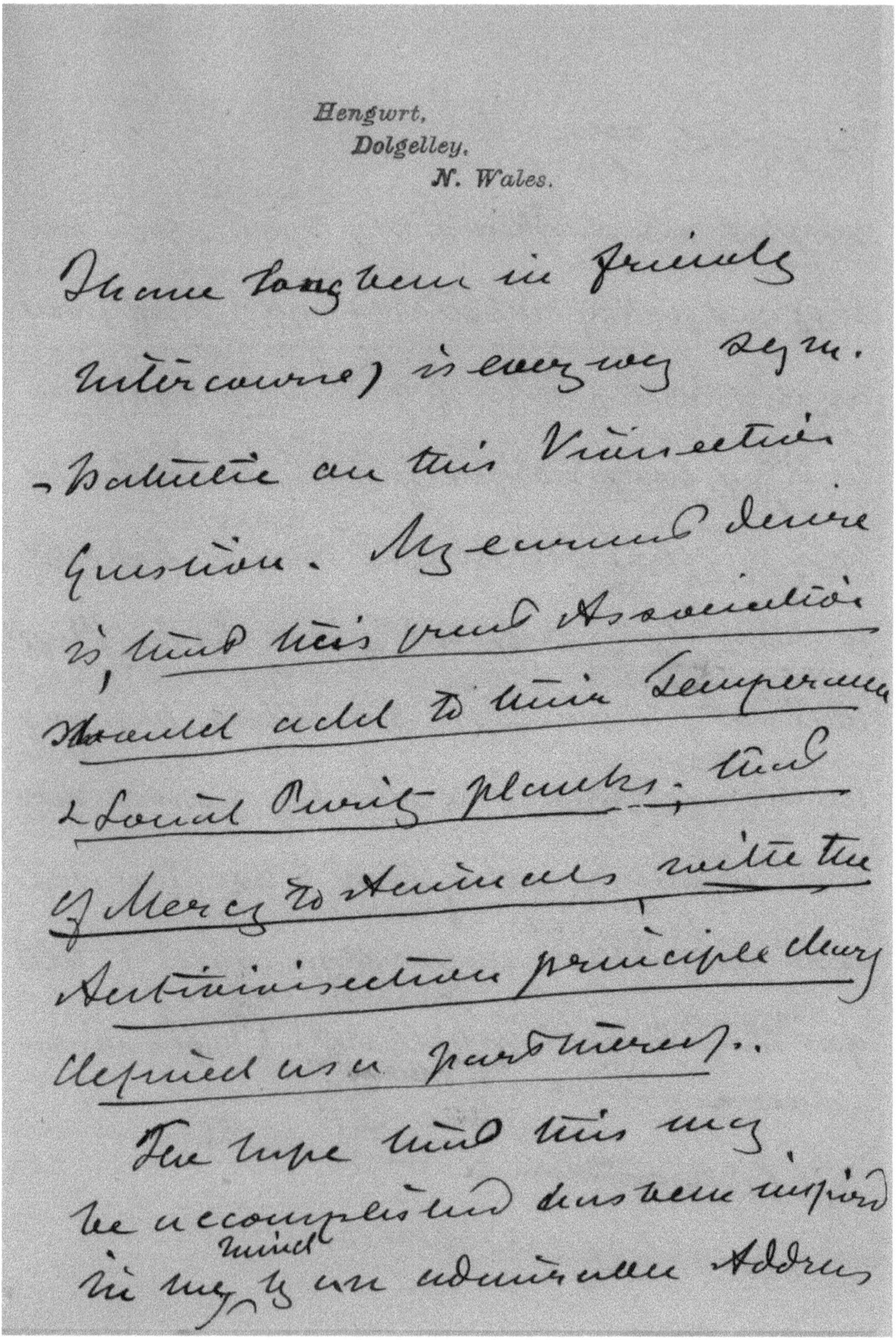

Hengwrt,
Dolgelley,
N. Wales.

I have long been in friendly
intercourse) in every way sym-
-pathetic on the Vivisection
Question. My earnest desire
is, that this great Association
should add to their Temperance
& Social Purity planks; that
of Mercy to Animals unite the
Antivivisection principle clearly
defined as a part thereof..

The hope that this may
be accomplished has been inspired
in my mind by an admirable Address

I have long been in friendly intercourse)
is everyway sympathetic on this Vivisection
question. My earnest desire is <u>that this</u>
<u>great Association would add to their</u>
<u>Temperance and Local Purity planks; that of</u>
<u>Mercy to Animals with the Antivivisection</u>
<u>principle clearly defined as a part thereof.</u>

The hope that this may be accomplished
was then imposed in my mind by an
admirable address

delivered recently by a Member of
the W.C.T.U., Mrs Lovell . of
Bryn Mawr, Montgomery Co Penn.
to a Branch of her Association.
I send you a copy which she
has sent me with, as interesting
& charming letters, expressing her
hope that the W.C.T.U. may take
up the matter, but explaining
that it will naturally take
some time to let the idea
filter through this immense
body so as to obtain intelligent

delivered recently by a member of the
W.C.T.U., Mrs. Lovell of Bergu Manor,
Montgomery 1ˢᵗ Penn. to a Branch of her
Association. I send you a copy which she
has sent me with 2 very interesting and
charming letters, expressing her hope that
the W.C.T.U. may take up the matter;
but experience knows it will naturally take
some time to let the idea filter through this
universe (in a) way so as to obtain intelligent

acceptance.

Miss Willard has likewise sent
me a copy of Mrs. Lovell's pamphlet
expressing her agreement with it &
saying the WCTU platform does include the
principle of mercy to animals.

I have sent Mrs. Lovell a little
money & some papers to help her
local propaganda; & have written
Miss Willard to implore her
to do whatever is possible to
carry out the idea; & have also
offered any number of thousands
of copies of "Light in Dark Places"
or this pamphlet for my papers
for distribution through the WCTU

acceptance.

Miss Willard has likewise sent me a copy of Mrs. Lovell's pamphlet expressing her appreciation with it and saying the W.C.T.U. platform _does_ include the principle of mercy to animals.

I have sent Mrs. Lovell a little money and some papers to help her local propaganda; I have written to Miss Willard to implore her to do whatever is possible to carry out the idea; I have also offered any number of thousands of copies of "Light in Dark Places" or other pamphlets she may prefer for distribution through the W.C.T.U.

You will now see, dear Mrs.
Pearsall Smith, exactly how things
stand, & will be able to judge where
& how you can help us, by urging
influential friends in America
either to join Mrs. White's League
(more particularly) to press the
various Branches of the WCTU
to take up the cause —
There is too great reason to fear that
Vivisection is carried on even more
recklessly & increasingly in America
than in England, & that the New Vice
(as I called) of Scientific Cruelty is being
instilled by education in numberless
Colleges throughout the Union — a fearful
prospect for the future! — I will not
trespass further on your patience.
Most truly & respectfully yrs
Frances Power Cobbe

You will now see, dear Mrs. Pearsall Smith, exactly how things stand and will be able to judge where and how you can help us <u>by urging influential friends in America either to join Mr. White's society or (more particularly) to press the various branches of the W.C.T.U. to take up the cause.</u>

There is too great remove to fear that vivisection is curious and even <u>more</u> reckless and merciless in America than in England, and thus the <u>New Vice</u> (as I call it) of scientific cruelty is being instilled by education in numberless colleges through most of the Union—A fearful prospect for the future! – I will end (...) further a (...)!

Most truly and respectfully yours,
Frances Power Cobbe

Note: The National Anti-Vivisection Society (NAVS) is the oldest anti-vivisection society in the world, first established by Francis Power Cobbe in 1875. It was originally called the Victoria Street Society and led directly to the Cruelty to Animals Act 1876. In 1898, the organization agreed to fight for lesser measures instead of the completeabolition of vivisection, which led to Frances Cobbe leaving the organization and founding the British Union for the Abolition of Vivisection. The NAVS continues to fight against animal testing for commercial, educational, or scientific purposes.

Biography

Ellice Hopkins (Oct. 30, 1836-Aug. 21, 1904)
(No image Available)

Jane Ellice Hopkins (Oct. 30, 1836-Aug. 21, 1904) was born in Cambridge and raised in an intellectual environment by her father, a geologist and mathematician and her mother, a musician. She was raised in a firm Church of England household and was quite religious. In the 1850's she worked as an evangelist and held Bible classes, but on the death of her father in 1866, she became involved in rescue work.

In her rescue work, Hopkins became involved with the Albion Hill Home for prostitutes and also met the medical doctor James Hinton, whose radical views on sexuality and his concern for women within the society influenced her. (She even edited a book on the *Life and Letters of James Hinton*.) In the process she was disturbed by Victorian sexual double standards, where women were blamed for "seducing" men and men were seen as incapable of self-restraint. She became a social reformer involved in the Purity Movement. In her early work she established the Soldier's Institute at Portsmouth in 1874, and worked to recruit women to the Ladies Association for the Care of Friendless Girls in 1876. She became an vital part of the promoting and passing of the Industrial Schools Amendment Act of 1880 to relocate children in brothels to approved reform schools, and the Criminal Law Amendment Act of 1885, which raised the age of sexual consent for girls from 13 to 16 years of age. She also wrote *A plea for the wider action of the Church of England in the prevention of the degradation of women* (1879) to confront this double standard, arguing the men needed to take responsibility for their own chastity.

In this work, she co-founded the White Cross Army in 1883 with Bishop Joseph Lightfoot of Durham, an organization of men committed to sexual purity before marriage and faithfulness in marriage. With this platform she eloquently addressed mass meetings of men about personal chastity and the sanctity of marriage and the Christian family. Her final book, *The Story of Life* (1902), was an innovative attempt to introduce early sex education. She also wrote poetry *English Idylls* (1865) and *Autumn Swallows* (1883), a novel, *Rose Turquand* (1876) and works to elevate the roles of women and emphasize purity: *An Englishwoman's Work among Workingmen* (1875), *Christ the Consoler, A Book of Comfort for the Sick* (1879), *True Manliness* (1884), and *The Power of Womanhood* (1899). She also wrote *Work in Brighton, or Women's Mission to Women* (1878) with Florence Nightingale.

(Note: Every page has writing in the marigins (reasoning as to why, our best guess is to conserve paper), this combined with the fact that the handwriting itself is bad, makes this particular work one of the hardest to read.)

2 Belle Vue Gardens, Brighton

April

Dear Mrs. Pearsall Smith,

Alas, some one has told you false. Mrs. Conklin is the Lecturer and Organizer of the W.C.T.U. generally, was unanimously reelected as such *last autumn* and yet they pursue her with their awful accusations and actually got her not placed on the list of speakers at the Purity Congress that

year at Chicago.
There is something
rotten in the state of
Denmark where these
things are possible
And I have just learned
from Dutton. That she
has made no effort
to pay the £12 ~ of
her debt to him since
last August when she
paid a small sum
the whole money
owing to him being
pushed into her
hands nearly a year
~ a half ago. Their
book having been

year at Chicago. There is something rotten in the state of Denmark where these things are possible. And I have just heard from Dutton that she has made no effort to pay the £12 remaining of her debt to him because last August when she paid a small sum the whole money owing to him dashing pieces into his hands nearly a year and a half ago. The book having been

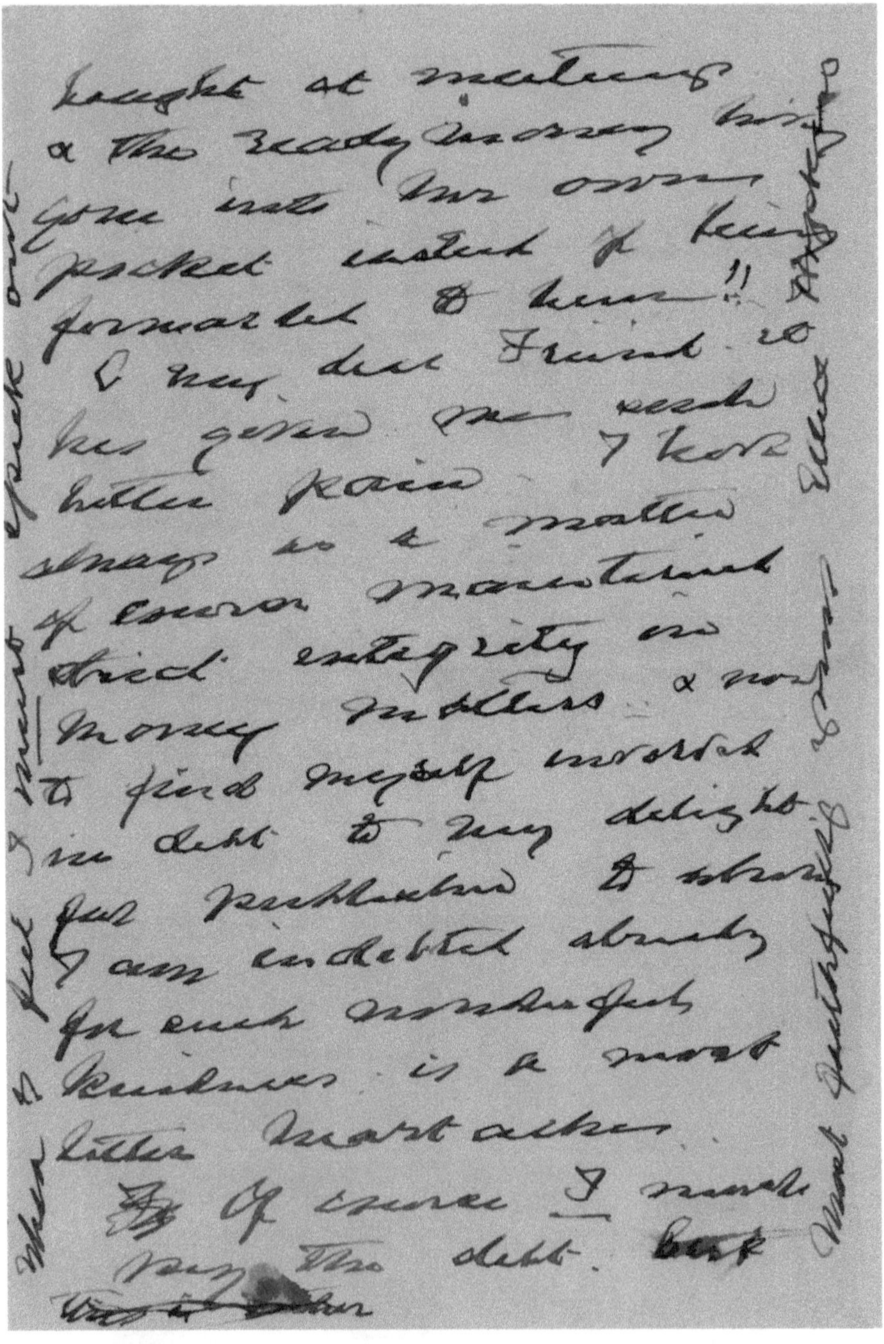
bought at meetings
& the ready money his
gone into his own
pocket instead of being
forwarded to him!!
O my dear Frank [illegible]
has given me such
bitter pain
always as a matter
of course maintained
strict integrity in
money matters & now
to find myself involved
in debt to my delight-
ful publishers to whom
I am indebted already
for such wonderful
kindness is a most
bitter mortification.
Of course I must
pay the debt. [illegible]
[illegible]

When I feel I must speak out

most distressing & [illegible]

bought at meetings and the ready money has gone into her own pocket instead of being forwarded to him!!

O. my dear friend it has given me such bitter pain. I have always as a matter of course maintained direct integrity in money matters and now to find myself involved in debt to my delightful publishers to whom I am indebted already for such wonderful kindness is a most bitter heartache.

Of course I must pay the debt

as I have the whole of our empire to work this [...] rather his own use.

For the present, I agree with you the best thing to do is to keep silence and <u>wait</u>. But in the end I shall have to speak in order to disassociate myself from her, as she uses my name everywhere and speaks of herself as my agent. And yet I have such intense reluctance to injure her W. X. [White Cross?] work though there again she is said to have pocketed fees given

. . . . . . The Rest of the Letter . . . .
(is located on pg. 146 written sideways and in the margins of the page)

. . . her for the month.

They never looked at her accounts or compared these with the accounts of the Y.M.C.A. who employed her. <u>No</u> attempt has been made to repay the accusation against her. The American work has been in [...] heartache and acts of others. At present keep silence. I will write when I feel I <u>must</u> speak out.

Most affectionately yours,
Ellice Hopkins

Charlotte Mason (Jan. 1, 1842-Jan. 16, 1923)
(Image in the Public Domain)

Biography

Charlotte Maria Shaw Mason (Jan. 1, 1842-Jan. 16, 1923) was born in Wales as an only child and as such her parents educated her at home. She became a teacher and taught for ten years in Worthing, England at Davison School. Worthing is about ten miles from Brighton, which is referenced in her letter. She also taught at the Bishop Otter Teacher Training College to help train governesses and co-founded the Parents' Educational Union (PEU), which was designed to help parents teach their children at home by providing resources. This later became the Parents' National Educational Union (PNEU).

Charlotte wrote a popular series of geography textbooks called the Ambleside Series from 1880 to 1892, but she is more known for her development of new educational methods for teaching young children. She published *Home Education* in 1886, as well as *Parents and Children* (1896), *School Education* (1904), and *Formation of Character* (1905) all outlining her philosophy of education. She also wrote the book *Ourselves* (1904) which was written directly to the children themselves to help them develop strong morals and discipline. She was the first educator to see the educational value of scouting in 1905, using Baden-Powell's book in her syllabus at the PEU. She also published *The Saviour of the World* (1904-1914), a six-volume account of the life of Jesus and what he taught, written in verse.

Mason's teaching philosophy and method argued that children should be seen as people in their own right, and that education must focus on the whole person. Her chief motto was "Education is an Atmosphere, a Discipline, a Life." She saw that children absorbed much of their knowledge from their home environment, or atmosphere, so that the rules lived out by the parents became a third of the child's education. By discipline, Mason meant the cultivation of good habits, especially in the child's character, which made up a second third of the child's education. The third part of a child's education should be made up of living knowledge, not just dry facts. So she encouraged students to explore nature, the arts, and subjects that interested them. Learning was accomplished by giving things our fullest attention and best efforts in a quest for knowledge that was the reward in itself.

Mason's final book was *Towards a Philosophy of Education* (1923), which revised and summed up her many years of thought and practice as an educator. It is often considered one of her best works and is still read by advocates of home schooling and educational theory.

Charlotte
Mason

HOUSE OF REST,
CAMBRIDGE GARDENS,
KILBURN, N.W.

Feb. 11. 1886

My dear Mrs Smith,

It was a great
pleasure to me, yesterday, to meet you
once more in England.
Those glorious meetings in
Brighton where I last
met you have borne
glorious fruit in my
experience and work,
and in that of hundreds.
if not thousands of others.

House of Rest
Cambridge Gardens
Kilburn, N.W.

Feb. 11, 1886

My dear Mrs. Smith,

It was a great pleasure to me yesterday to meet you once more in England. Those glorious meetings in Brighton where I had met you have become glorious fruit in my experience and work, and in that of hundreds if not thousands of others.

The devil was never likely
to let a movement like
that pass unchallenged,
and he had no difficulty
in finding instruments for
his work in timid half-
hearted Christians.
But all the hubbub made
no difference to me. The
Lord revealed himself
to me at that time, although
I had been a Christian
and a worker for years.
and the revelation con-
tinues "a living bright

The devil was never likely to let a moment like that pass unchallenged, and he had no difficulty in finding instruments for his work in timid half-hearted Christians.

But all that hubbub made no difference to me. The Lord revealed Himself to me at that time, although I had been a Christian and a worker for years, and the resolution continues " a living bright

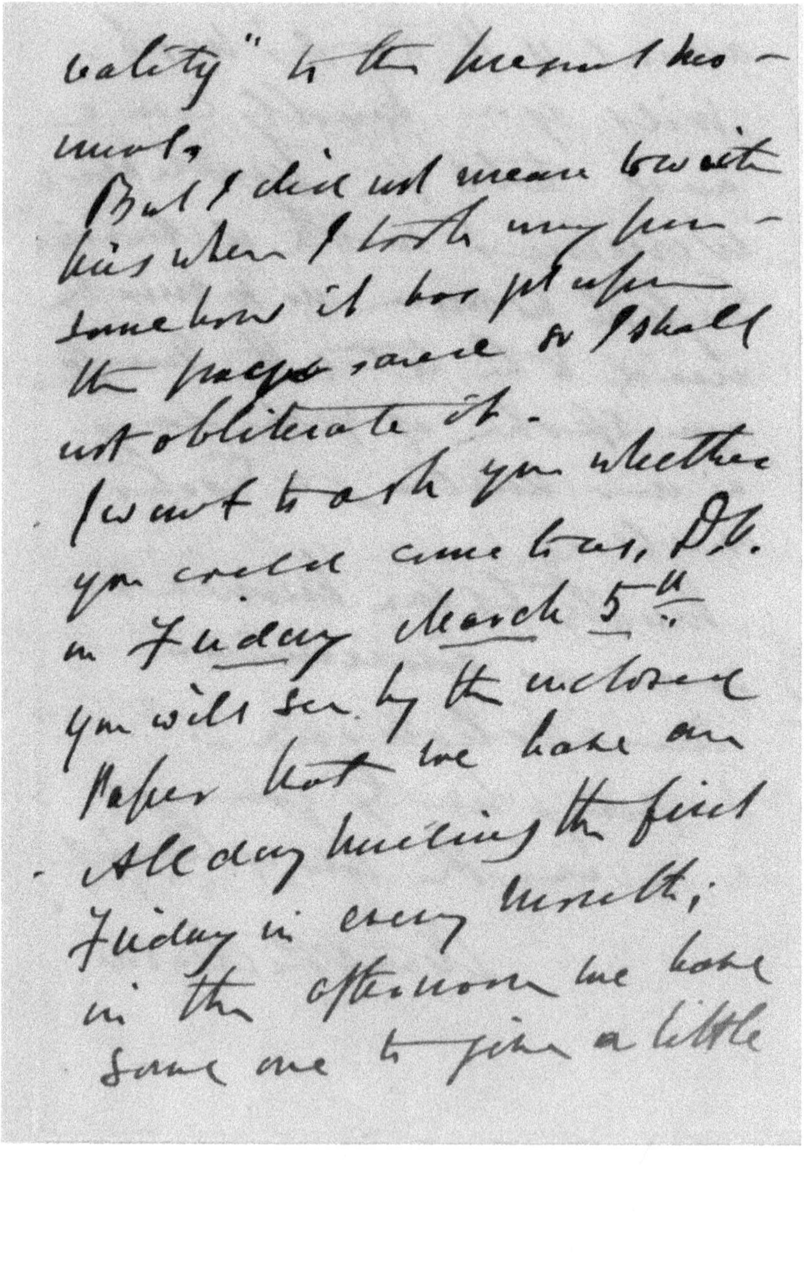
"vality" to the present mo-
ment.
But I did not mean to write
this when I took my pen -
somehow it has got upon
the paper since & I shall
not obliterate it.
I want to ask you whether
you could come to us, D.V.
on Friday March 5th.
You will see by the enclosed
paper that we have an
All day meeting the first
Friday in every month;
in the afternoon we have
some one to give a little

reality" to the present moment.

But I did not mean to write this when I took my pen—somehow it has got upon the page and so I shall not obliterate it.

I want to ask you whether you could come to us. D.C. on Friday March 5th. You will see by the enclosed paper that we have an all day meeting the first Friday in every month; in the afternoon we have some one to give a little account of the Lord's work.

Will you kindly come
and tell the people about
Woman's work in America.
English women do so much
need to be told the things
you spoke of yesterday
in our meeting in Exeter
Hall—

Kindly let me know as
soon as convenient—
And believe me,
very truly yours,
in the love of Christ.

Charlotte Mason.

account of the Lord's work. Will you kindly come and tell the people about Woman's Work in America? English women do so much need to be told the things you spoke of yesterday in the meeting in Seaton Hall.

Kindly let me know as soon as convenient, and believe me very truly yours in the love of Christ,

Charlotte Mason

Part Five: Civil Rights

"One dear woman that I met last fall at the Saturday night holiness meeting, told me she was converted at that meeting: also her husband and two children. She told me how she disliked me because I was a colored woman: how she went to church full of prejudice, but when God saved her He took it all out, and now she loves me as a sister and thinks I have a beautiful color! Of course I call that a good conversation to begin with. Some people don't get enough of the blessing to take prejudice out of them, even after they are sanctified."

-Amanda Smith

An Autobiography: The Story of the Lord's Dealings with Mrs. Amanda Smith, the Colored Evangelist: Containing an Account of Her Life Work of Faith, and Her Travels in America, England, Ireland, Scotland, India, and Africa as an Independent Missionary (1893), page 226.

Amelia Stone Quinton (July 31, 1833-June 23, 1926)
(Image in the Public Domain)

Biography

Amelia Stone Quinton (July 31, 1833-June 23, 1926) grew up in a Baptist family in New York State. She was deeply religious and was often involved in charitable work with the poor and prisoners. She also taught for a year in a Georgia seminary. In 1874 she joined the Women's Christian Temperance Union and was the state organizer until 1877. After a brief visit to Britain, she married Rev. Richard L. Quinton of London and settled down in Philadelphia. In 1879 she visited a friend of hers, Mary Lucinda Bonney, who she knew from her time as a teacher. From Bonney she learned that there were political moves to open Indian Territory for white settlement, in violation of earlier treaties.

Quinton and Bonney became active in raising awareness of this move to violate the treaties with Native Americans. They collected thousands of signatures and Quinton called on Congress to develop a new federal Indian policy that would provide free education, grant Native Americans citizenship, help make Native Americans equal before the law, and provide land to Native Americans. By 1883 Quinton and Bonney formed the Women's National Indian Association. Through working with other Indian rights associations, Quinton was instrumental in the passing of the Dawes General Allotment Act.

Sadly, the Dawes General Allotment Act, established with the best of intentions, did much to negatively affect Native Americans. It provided for Native Americans to become citizens and get allotments of land for farming, but in order to pass Congress, a compromise also allowed whites a chance to purchase Native American land as well. Quinton and others of her day, saw the best hope of Native Americans was to become like white society, and so this move meant to protect Native American land and give them citizenship, also resulted in a loss of land and an increasing loss of community and culture. Mission schools also played a negative role in this process until changes in federal Indian policy in the 1930's. While recognizing these negative results, it is also important to remember that without Quinton and Bonney, it is very likely that much more Native American territory would have been taken by laws Congress was considering, and neither citizenship, equality before the law, or funds for education were considered for compensation.

In 1901, the Women's National Indian Association allowed men to join and became the National Indian Association, working for Native American rights. Amelia Quinton went on to found some fifty missions among Native Americans providing resources to build homes, provide teachers, and establish libraries on reservations. In a time when most white Christians had little concern for Native American issues, Amelia Stone Quinton stands as a shining example of a Christian concerned for diversity and equal rights for Native Americans.

Amelia S. Quinton

Bless you Darling
For all your
lovely letters & work
& [etc] all your goodness
to me. You have
blessed me & cheered
me fainting many
a time but never
so much as now in
this emergency. Heart
failing with domestic
grief & this new place
of care & now you stand
by me solidly & I do
bless you for it. It helps
us you can't realize
unless you had been in
my place. Your spoken

Bless you darling,

For all your lovely letters and work and for all your goodness to me. You have blessed me and cheered me fainting many a time but never so much as now in this emergency. Heart failing with domestic griefs and this new place of care and now you _stand by me solidly_ and I do bless you for it. It helps us you can't realize unless you had been in my place. Your _spoken_

trust, confidence, kindness
pull me up out of the
depths & make me
feel I can go on. Dear
Saint Miriam! She is
an angel. God bless
her. He will! He does!

I hope to see you
next week, just off for
Morristown meeting, Am
guest of the ex Gov. Randolph
there. God does uphold.

All love ever to thee
my own precious
beloved Sister from

Thy Aunty,

Newark N. J.
Yours! Oct 2 '87.

trust, confidence, kindness pull me up out of the depths and make me feel I <u>can</u> go on. Dear saint Miriam! <u>She</u> is an angel. God bless <u>her</u>. He will! He does!

I hope to see you next week. Just off for Morristown meeting. Am guest of the ex Gov. Randolph there. God <u>does</u> uphold.

All love ever to thee my own precious beloved sister from,

Thy Amy (Amelia Stone Quinton)

Newark, NY

Thurs. Oct. 26. 1887

Amanda Smith (Jan. 23, 1837-Feb. 24, 1915)
(Image in the Public Domain)

Biography

Amanda Berry Smith (Jan. 23, 1837-Feb. 24, 1915) was born into slavery in Long Green, Maryland. Her father was an incredibly hard worker who earned money after completing his daily work in order to purchase his freedom and that of his wife and thirteen children. The family then settled in Pennsylvania, where Amanda's parents taught her to read and write at home. Amanda eventually went to work as a servant and washerwoman for a white family. Smith was married twice, but lost both husbands early, one being killed in the Civil War, and four of her five children dying before she was 32 years old.

To help with her grief she turned to the African Methodist Episcopal Church and became known for her singing voice and her teaching. She dressed simply and was widely received in religious camp meetings and revivals. She was heard by both white and African-American audiences and would ultimately become known as "God's image carved in ebony."

With her growing fame in Methodist and Holiness circles, Smith was invited to Europe where she attended the Broadlands Conference of the Mount Temples and also continued preaching in England for two years. From there she travelled to India where she taught for 18 months, and then she journeyed to Africa where she spent eight years in Liberia and West Africa. She returned to the United States and continued her ministry, while also writing an influential autobiography. Rev. Charles Mason, the founder of the Church of God in Christ, the largest African-American Pentecostal denomination in the U.S., credited this book for teaching him the doctrine of sanctification.

In 1899, Amanda Smith founded the Amanda Smith Orphanage and Industrial Home for Abandoned and Destitute Colored Children near Chicago. Due to fire and financial problems it closed in 1917, two years after Amanda Smith passed away in Sebring, Florida.

While there is no letter in the collection from Amanda Smith, she relates her encounter with Robert Pearsall Smith and Hannah Whitall Smith in her autobiography. While she doesn't explicitly say, Hannah's influence may also explain Amanda Smith's gracious welcome to the Broadlands Conference by the Mount Temples on her later trip to Europe in 1879. Amanda Smith writes,

> Again it was in 1870 or 1871, when my dear friend, Mrs. Hannah Whitehall Smith, was holding those marvelous Bible readings in Germantown and Philadelphia that God blessed so wonderfully. I had often heard them spoken of, and read of them, and thought how I would like to go; but then I did not know whether they would allow colored persons to go. The Lord would often send me around among white people where there was a good meeting going on, that I might learn more perfectly some lesson from His Word.

> One day I was on my way to West Philadelphia when Mr. Robert Pearson Smith, who had been off in California, doing some evangelistic work, I believe, and had got home just a few days before, got on the car, and after he had sat down a little while he looked over and recognized me. He came and said, "I think this is Amanda Smith?" I said, "Yes." He took a seat by me, and did not have any fear or embarrassment from my being a colored woman. How real, and kind, and true he was. He said, "Amanda Smith, has thee attended any of the meetings that my wife, Hannah, has been holding?"

> "No," I said, "I have thought I would like so much to go, but I did not know if they would allow colored persons to go."

> "Oh, yes, Amanda," he said, "there would be no objection to thee going, and I think thee would enjoy the meeting very much. God has wonderfully blessed Hannah, and scores of ladies of rank have been led to consecrate themselves to the Lord, and have realized great blessing. She will hold a meeting at 1018 Arch street, on Friday. Thee must go."

> I thanked him very kindly, and told him I would do so.

> "Now," I thought to myself, "the Lord has answered my prayer and opened the way for me, and no doubt He has some blessed lesson to teach me from His Word; for Mrs. Smith is such a wonderful Bible teacher."

> So I looked forward to Friday with great delight. When the day came I got ready and went, prayerfully. But somehow I seemed to have a little trembling come over me as I neared the corner of Tenth and Arch streets; and I said to myself, "I wonder what is going to happen: my heart has become so sad all in a moment."

Then I began to pray more earnestly that the Lord would help me and lead me. Sometimes these feelings of sadness, thought unexplainable, are the omen of a great blessing from God; at another time they may indicate disappointment and sadness, so that in either case God permits them, and prepares the heart by prayer to receive the blessing, or to endure the sorrow or disappointment. Praise His name for this.

Just when I was about to turn the corner, I saw two ladies coming. I knew them, and they were on the way to the meeting. I thought, "I will let them pass, and I will follow on close behind, and go in just when they are fairly in." I always try to avoid anything like pushing myself, or going where I was not wanted. And then I knew how sensititve many white people are about a colored person, so I always kept back. I don't think that anybody can ever say that Amanda Smith pushed herself in where she was not wanted. I was something like the groundhog; when he sees his shadow he goes in; I always could see my shadow far enough ahead to keep out of the way. But I thought as Mr. Pearson Smith had so kindly told me that it would be all right for me to go to this meeting, that I would not be intruding; no, certainly not. When these ladies got up to me, they stopped, and spoke to me very kindly; they said, "Well, Amanda Smith, how does thee do? Is thee going to the meeting?"

"Yes," I said, "I have heard and read a good deal about the meeting, and I thought I would go to-day."

I saw they looked a little nervous or queer, so I said to them, "I met Mr. Pearson Smith the other day, and he told me to go; there would be no objection, and the meetings were very wonderful in blessing, and he thought I would enjoy them."

"Well, Amanda," one of the ladies said, "the meeting will be very full to-day, and there will be a great many very wealthy ladies in from Germantown, and West Philadelphia, and Walnut Hills, and the meetings are especially for this class, and I think thee had better not go to-day; some other day would be better for thee." And then they politely bowed, and went on.

I never said a word. I was dumbfounded; and there I stood. I thought, "How is this? I have been praying about this meeting ever since I saw Mr. Smith, and I have been expecting a real feast to my soul to-day, and now these ladies feel it won't do for me to go, because I am a colored woman, and so many of the wealthy ladies will be there. They don't know but that the Lord may have sent a message to some of them through me." So I said, "I will linger about till I know the meeting is well begun, then I will go and stand at the door."

Now I felt in my heart it was right to do this instead of going back home. I did so. "And after all it may be I may hear the word the Lord has for me; for He meant something by my coming." So I slipped in quietly and stood at the door; there were a number of others standing up. Just as Mrs. Smith was in the midst of her good Bible address, sure enough the Lord had a message for me, and I got a great blessing as I stood at the door. Praise the Lord!

And now, the change is, instead of Amanda Smith, the colored washwoman's presence having a bad effect on a meeting where ladies of wealth and rank are gathered to pray and sing His blessing, they think a failure more possible if the same Amanda Smith, the colored woman, cannot be present. This is all the Lord's doings, and marvelous in our eyes.

At the close of this meeting as the ladies were passing out, one and another came to me and spoke to me, and shook hands; "Why, this is Amanda Smith."

"Yes."

"Oh, here is Amanda Smith; why didn't you sing?" And another, "Oh I have heard of you." And another, "Oh, I wish you had sung such a piece." And another, "Why didn't you speak?" And another, "I have heard you sing such a piece at Ocean Grove at such a time, or at Round Lake." I was glad of this, for I thought, "After all, I have not spoiled the spirit of the meeting."

But then, I was not so well known then, and many people were shy of me, and are yet. But I belong to Royalty, and am well acquainted with the King of Kings, and am better known and better understood among the great family above than I am on earth. But I thank God the time is coming, and we "Shall know each other better when the mists have rolled away." Hallelujah! Amen.

(*An Autobiography: The Story of the Lord's Dealings with Mrs. Amanda Smith the Colored Evangelist*, by Mrs. Amanda Smith, 1893, pages 196-198)

Olive Schreiner (Mar. 24, 1855–Dec. 11, 1920)
(Image in the Public Domain)

Biography

Olive Emilie Albertina Schreiner (Mar. 24, 1855-Dec. 11, 1920) was born on the Eastern Cape of South Africa to missionary parents from the Wesleyan Missionary Society. With the failure of the mission and subsequent business ventures, Schreiner had a difficult life often living with siblings as she was educated. She became a governess to support herself, but often had conflicts with those who hired her. From her exposure to her very religious family, Schreiner rejected traditional religious doctrines for an intellectual belief in an agnostic Absolute and her own view of morality separate from organized religion. She suffered strong asthma attacks most of her life.

From 1881-1889 Schreiner lived in England becoming involved with various freethinkers and their organizations. On her return to South Africa, she opposed Cecil Rhodes for his "strop bill" that permitted black and colored servants to be beaten for minor offences. She argued against the Boer War and hoped for a non-racist, non-sexist South Africa. Schreiner became the vice-president of the Women's Enfranchisement League in 1907, but withdrew her support when the organization refused to include black women in the right to vote. In her later years she worked with other activists against World War I as a pacifist.

Olive Schreiner was perhaps best known as an author, the first major fiction writer from South Africa. Her novel, *The Story of an African Farm* (1883) is a semi-autobiographical story interwoven with views of free thought, feminism, and philosophy. Her work *Trooper Peter Halket of Mashonland* (1897) was written as a satirical response to Cecil Rhodes and the "strop bill." *Woman and Labour* (1911) presents her concerns with socialism and the equal treatment of women. Two uncompleted works were finished after her death; *From Man to Man* (1926) is considered one of her finest works about racism and feminism in South Africa, and *Undine* (1929), which was actually one of her first written manuscripts.

Xmas Hill
Olive   Wednesday
(Olive) Schreiner

Dear Mrs Smith
                    I thank you
it would have
been lovely & I
should certainly
have come, only
I have got to go
down to Brighton
tomorrow. My
cottage has been

Imap Hill
Weleeselly

Dear Mrs. Smith,

Thank you, it would have been lovely
and I should certainly have come, only I
have got to go down to Brighton tomorrow.
My cottage has been

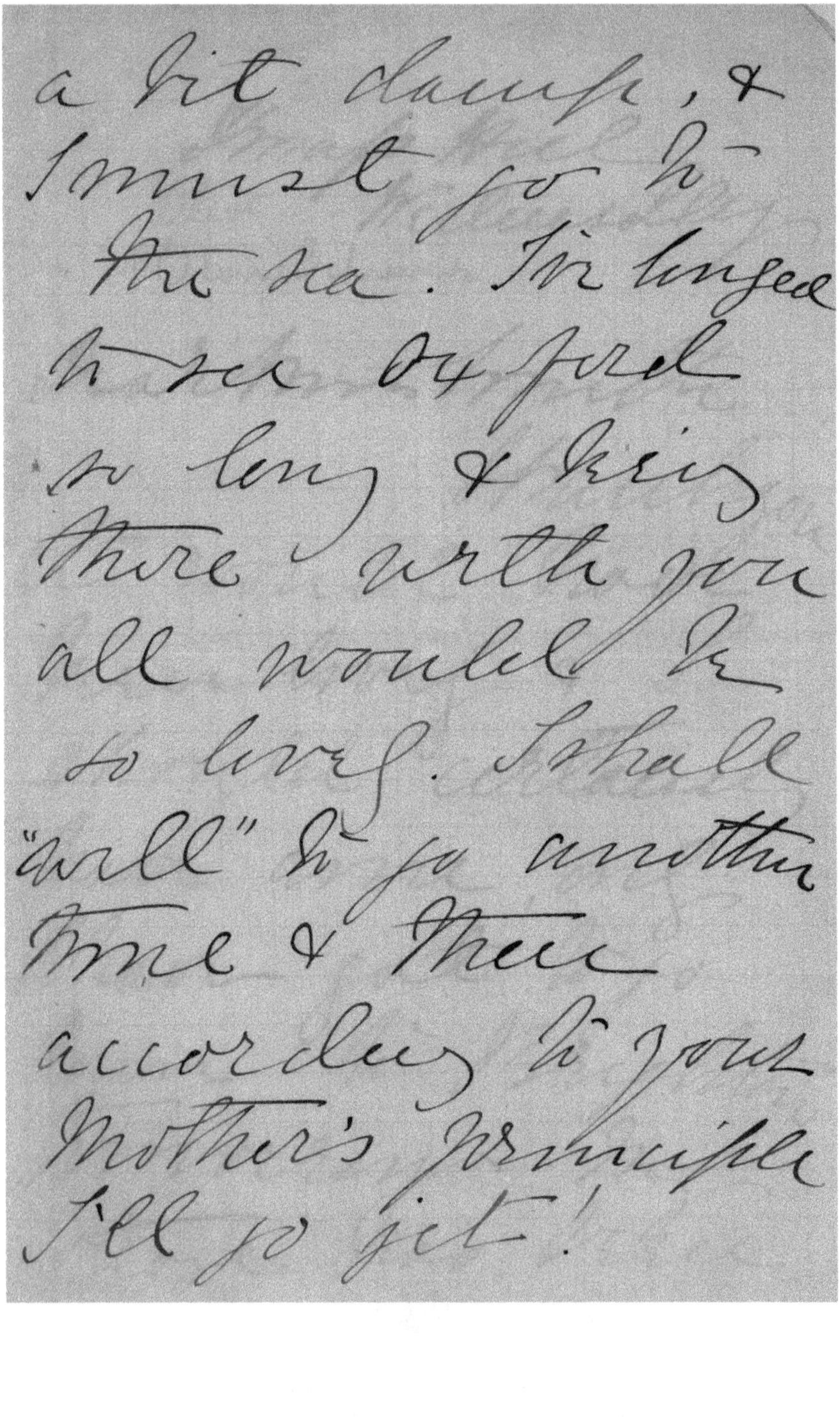

a bit damp and I must go to the sea. I've longed to see Oxford so long and being there with you all would be so lovely. I shall "will" to go another time and then according to your Mother's principle I'll go jet!

2

I can just fairly
I see the two small
people in their
white "nappies."
You will come
down with her
to Brighton some
day to see me
won't you? &
she can go in
a goat carriage
& we'll bathe!
My address will

I can just fairly I see the two small people in their white "kappyes." You will come down with her to Brighton some day to see me won't you? And she can go in a goat carriage and we'll bathe!

My address will

(Or 27) Medina Villas
West Brighton.
It's almost quite
at the end of
the term on the
Downs. It was
so good of you
to think of asking
me to Oxford.
I hope you'll
enjoy it. Remember
me to your brother.
Yours always
Olive Schreiner

be 27 Medina Villas, West Brighton. Its almost quite at the end of the town on the Downs. It was so good of you to think of asking me to Oxford. I hope you'll enjoy it. Remember me to your mother.

Yours always,
Olive Schreiner

Anna Spafford (Mar. 16, 1842–Apr. 17, 1923)
(Image in the Public Domain)

Biography

Anne Tobine Larsdatter Øglende (Spafford) (Mar. 16, 1842-Apr. 18, 1923) was born in Stavanger, Norway. Her carpenter father and Anne immigrated to Chicago in 1846, living the poor life of many immigrant families. On September 5, 1861 the young Norwegian immigrant, now called Anna, married Horatio Gates Spafford, a young Chicago lawyer and devout Evangelical. He was a close friend of Dwight Moody before Moody rose to fame as an evangelist. The young couple rose in wealth and popularity, and soon had a family of four daughters. Their house survived the infamous Chicago fire in 1871, but this disaster began to unravel some of Horatio's dubious financial speculations. Anna and her daughters were sent to France in November of 1873 aboard the luxury vessel, the *S.S. Ville de Havre*. In the worst disaster of its day, the Ville de Havre sunk in icy water losing 232 lives including all four of the Spafford's daughters, the youngest being pulled from her mother's arms by the waves. Anna was found unconscious floating on a piece of wreckage the next day. Her telegram to her husband read simply, "Saved alone."

This event radically changed the couple's life. Anna had not been strongly religious, but even Dwight Moody coming to her side in England after the rescue could not give her the answers she sought. Horatio took a boat to Europe and somewhere near where his four daughters drowned, he composed the famous hymn, "It is well with my soul." While this hymn became a mainstay in many Evangelical hymnbooks, Horatio was undergoing his own religious trial. He began to develop theological ideas outside the norm of Evangelicalism, including the belief that all would be ultimately saved, including Satan, and none would go to hell. Anna and Horatio became very interested in premillennialism and determined that Christ was to return very shortly in Jerusalem. They began to build a small community known as the Overcomers in Chicago, led by Horatio and his sister, Maggie Lee, who had experienced a form of sanctification in a Methodist Camp meeting, and determined that she was a prophetess.

Hannah Whitall Smith visited the group when they were in Chicago, out of a genuine interest in their experience. They later visited her in Pennsylvania and tried to convince her to join them. She wrote about them in her notes on Religious Fanaticism, and chose not to join them, but she retained a keen interest in the Spaffordites.

Led by the prophecies of Mrs. Lee, the teachings of Horatio, and rapidly unraveling financial situations in Chicago, a group of 16 of the Overcomers left Chicago and arrived in Jerusalem in 1881. They believed the Second Coming was imminent, so they did very little work, lived on borrowed money, and held that they were the remnant of the true believers who would greet Christ on His return. They won the hearts of many Jews and Muslims because they did not try to convert them, but freely and equally shared what they had to help the poor and the sick. By 1888, Horatio died. Negative publicity in the U.S., huge financial indebtedness, along with the enmity of the U.S. Consul in Jerusalem resulted in a huge crisis. The Overcomers buried their dead in a small American cemetery, but with no headstones, since the dead were soon to be raised anyway. Anna now took control of the Overcomers, who were also known as "The American Colony." Under her guidance, the community began to work, operated as a commune, for a long period of time with chastity as the rule and all marriages disbanded. A large influx of new believers came from Sweden. The American Colony sold items to tourists, used their community as a hotel, and still worked hard in caring for the poor and the sick, winning the friendship of Jews and Muslims alike. Under Anna's guidance the community thrived and became a vibrant part of the Jerusalem of its day. They stayed through the collapse of the Ottoman Empire, World War I, and through plagues and sectarian violence, waiting for the return of Christ.

The American Colony only survived a few years after the death of Anna Spafford, but the descendants of the original community still own the five-star American Colony Hotel in Jerusalem and the Spafford Children's Center still provides care for both Jewish and Muslim children equally.

This letter is in reply to one I wrote asking about them. I confess I cannot make much out of it.

Jerusalem Jan 17. 1900

Dear Mrs Smith;—

At the time your letter arrived I was so occupied that I felt I could not reply to it as I wished, so sent you a Postal Card & a few Photographs which I hope you received.

I remember very well the time you allude to when several of our company stopped at your house, & also the kind & hospitable spirit in which you received them.

You say "At that time Mrs Lee seemed to be the leader of the overcomers, but I have since heard that you have taken her place."

I hardly know where to begin to tell you of the wonderful dealings of God with us. God called us, as I believe He did & has done with many others,

(Note: Hannah writes, *"This letter is in reply to one I wrote asking about them. I confess I cannot make much out of it."*)

Jerusalem Jan. 17. 1900

Dear Mrs. Smith:

At the time your letter arrived I was so occupied that I felt I could not reply to it as I wished, so sent you a Postal Card and a few photographs which I hope you received.

I remember very well the time you allude to when several of our company stopped at your house, and also the kind and hospitable spirit in which you received them.

You say "At that time Mrs. Lee seemed to be the leader of the overcomers, but I have since heard that you have taken her place."

I hardly know where to begin to tell you of the wonderful dealings of God with us. God called us, as I believe He did and has done with many others.

to live a holy life, impressing us with the fact that He was a just & _real_ God, & His word just as _real_ as Himself. We were a very blind & stupid people—like children in a kinder garten—& He had to take us thro' many manifestations & object-lessons to penetrate us with the reality of His word,—so intoxicated were we with the wine of unfaithful worship that, now, as we look back upon the beginning of this call of God to us, we can see how deeply we were in the letter of things, without understanding the spirit of the Father nor His Son, & thinking that God would be satisfied with His Son's obedience instead of ours, thus releasing us from all fellowship except as by proxy.

God at that time took several of us to represent principles, the principles of to live a holy life, impressing us with the fact that He was a just and _real_ God, and His word just as _real_ as Himself. We were a very blind and stupid people—like children in a kinder garden and He had to take us thro' many manifestations and object lessons to penetrate us with the reality of His word, so intoxicated were we with the wine of unfaithful worship that, now, as we look back upon the beginning of this call of God to us, we can see how deeply we were in the _letter_ of things without understanding the Spirit of the Father nor His Son, and thinking that God would be satisfied with His Son's obedience instead of ours, thus releasing us from all fellowship except as by proxy.

God at that time took several of us to represent principles, the principles of

the Spirit which must be born out of
unity: this was a world perfectly new
to us & all we could do was to give God an
honest desire & a pure motive for righteousness,
leaving ourselves as clay in His hands.
Thro' this stage of blind faith & darkness we
emerged into light & an understanding
of God's will for man, & the Spirit of His Son
which must pervade us, in order that we
might have fellowship in the unity existing
between the Father & the Son. It was made
clear to us that we must have fellowship
with the truth in order to realize the
deep enmity against it, & thro' this to
understand the deep depravity of the
human heart; this we found levelled
every thing & forever dispelled the assumption
of leadership, & gave us to understand
to the full, the meaning of His oft repeated
expression that He was "Son of man"

the Spirit which must be born out of unity: this way
a world perfectly new to us and all _we_ could do was
to give God an honest desire and a pure motive for
righteousness leaving ourselves as clay in His hands.
Thro' this stage of blind faith and darkness we emerged
into light and an understanding of God's will for man,
and the Spirit of His Son which must pervade us,
in order that we might have fellowship in the unity
existing between the Father and the Son. It was made
clear to us that we must have _fellowship_ with the
truth in order to realize the deep enmity against it,
and thro' this to understand the deep depravity of
the human heart; this we found leveled everything
and forever dispelled the assumption of leadership and
gave us to understand to the full, the meaning of
it's oft-repeated expression that He was "Son of Man."

Standing in this place one experiences the
different principles of evil in man, which Satan
uses to overthrow one, - as represented by Judas
who would make merchandize of God's word,
& Peter who was ashamed to be connected
with the truth, & Thomas, who while he believed
that It was from God, disbelieved the power
of God to raise the truth after man had so
effectually, as he thought, destroyed it, - &
the spirit of the Jews who would not give up
place or nation to the truth, - & of the cruel
persecution which followed the Saints
after It.   Who of us could endure to
meet all this? Who could endure to hold to
that Holy Spirit of God that convicted of sin
& of judgment & of righteousness, until
Satan had exhausted all his power
upon them? Who of us could endure
to be misunderstood & to be called
Spiritualists & devils, & have every device

Standing in this place one experiences the different principles of evil in man, which Satan uses to overthrow one, as represented by Judas who would make merchandise of God's word, and Peter who was ashamed to be connected with the truth, and Thomas, who while he believed that It was from God, disbelieved the power of God to raise the truth after man had so effectually, as he thought, destroyed it, and the Spirit of the Jews who would not give up place or nation to the truth, and of the cruel persecution which followed the Saints after It. Who of us could endure to meet all this? Who could endure to hold to that Holy Spirit of God that convicted of sin and of judgment and of righteousness, until Satan had exhausted all his power upon them? Who of us could endure to be misunderstood and to be called spiritualists and devils and have every device

of Satan hurled against them, & many
thinking they were doing God service to
denounce us, until we appeared like
the filth of all the earth? Who of us
could believe that thro' all this the truth
would rise again? Who of us could
endure this to an end until one
came into fellowship with the Spirit
of It when He said "Father forgive them
for they know not what they do"? Thus
proving that the enmity that came in
with the fall was nailed to the cross!
This has been the career of this work
& we who remain at this day have
experienced these things.
You say "I remember at that time the
Overcomer is expected It to come for his
Bride very short G; is that belief still
held & if so, how do you account for
the delay?" We do still hold that belief

of Satan hurled against them, and many thinking they were doing God's service to denounce us, until we appeared like the filth of all the earth? Who of us could believe that thro' all this the truth would rise again? Who of us could endure this to an end until one came into fellowship with the Spirit of It when He said "Father forgive them for they know not what they do"? Thus proving that the enmity that came in with the fall was nailed to the cross! This has been the career of this work and we who remain at this day have experienced these things.

You say "I remember at that time the overcomers expected It to come for His Bride very shortly; is that belief still held and, if so, how do you account for the delay?" We do still hold that belief

and that when there is a Bride, which
is unity, It will come, — to us there has been
no delay, any more than there was to It
who could not go to the Father until He had
finished the work which the Father had given
Him to do. Abraham could not have explained
to his fellowmen the reason why God had
called him to be a great nation, he could
only say God has promised me a son, &
he saw no reason why Ishmael could
not be taken & God begin at once to make
him a great nation, but the point was
not the great nation but the faith & patience
which would make him an heir, according to God's order, to the promise; after
which he could explain all, having come
to understand God's plan by enduring
to go thro' God's word.

You say that Mrs Lee when you met
her, was writing a new Bible, under, as

and that when there is a Bride, which is unity, It will come, to us there has been no delay, any more than there was to It who could not go to the Father until He had finished the work which the Father had given Him to do. Abraham could not have explained to his fellowmen the reason why God had called him to be a great nation, he could only say God has promised me a son and he saw no reason why Ishmael could not be taken and God begin at once to make him a great nation, but the point was not the great nation but the _faith_ and _patience_ which would make him an heir, according to God's order, to the promise, after which he could explain all, having come to understand God's plan by enduring to go thro' God's word.

You say that Mrs. Lee when you met her "was writing a new Bible, under, as

she believed divine inspiration": this was
never so. What I have written to you now,
& what we have experienced, was what God
opened to Mrs Lee at that time. It truly
was to us a new commandment, & yet
it was the old. I never heard Mrs Lee
call it a new Bible.

God revealed to Mrs Lee that unless, like
the kernel of wheat, we fell into the ground
& died we remained alone. You may
say we all know that. So did we, but—
when we came to live it & have fellowship
with It in it, we tasted of the enmity against
the truth, which in no other way could
we know, as before stated.

God also revealed to Mrs Lee, how
in meeting God in His Word, His
righteous requirement would be made
manifest, & all the world would be
brought to Him.

she believed divine inspiration." This was never so. What I have written to you now, and what we have experienced was what God opened to Mrs. Lee at that time. It truly was to us a <u>new</u> commandment, and yet it was <u>the old</u>. I never heard Mrs. Lee call it a new Bible.

God revealed to Mrs. Lee that unless like the kernel of wheat, we fell into the ground and died we remained alone. You may say we all know <u>that</u>. So did we, but when we came to live it and have fellowship with It in it, we tasted of the enmity against the truth, which in no other way could we know, as before stated.

God also revealed to Mrs. Lee how in meeting God in His Word, His righteous requirement would be made manifest and all the world would be brought to Him.

God showed Mrs Lee at that time that man had rejected the <u>overcoming</u> or chief corner stone, which must be made the head of the corner.

Mrs Lee died about 8 years ago. When Mrs Lee saw what the truth that God was giving her cost, she trembled, — but her faith that it was God's work, was never shaken. She realized that it cost all that we had & feared that few of us would endure to meet; but those of us who remain, counted the cost from the beginning, & with joy have met the trials & discipline which God sent to perfect us. The U. S. Consul here & our friends united their forces to starve & scatter us, with such relentless persistent that they did not hesitate even to mutilate the remains of our dead. We number today 150 souls. The Mahometans & Jews respect us & wonder at the power which enables us to live in harmony & peace.

God showed Mrs. Lee at that time that man had rejected the overcoming or chief cornerstone, which must be made the head of the corner.

Mrs. Lee died about 8 years ago. When Mrs. Lee saw what the truth that God was giving her cost, she trembled, but her faith that it was God's work, was never shaken. She realized that it cost all that we had and feared that few of us would endure to meet it: but those of us who remain, counted the cost from the beginning, and with joy have met the trials of discipline which God sent to perfect us. The U.S. Consul here and our friends united their forces to starve and scatter us, with such relentless persistent that they did not hesitate even to mutilate the remains of our dead. We number today 150 souls.

The Mahometans and Jews respect us and wonder at the power which enables us to live in harmony and peace.

Mrs Gould, who with Mrs Lee stayed with you at Germantown, wishes to be remembered to you.

The picture I sent you shewing part of the city wall & a section of the houses in Jerusalem, shews as the highest house within the walls, one of the houses we occupy.

It is difficult for me to go into details respecting this work, for I could fill volumes. I have tried to give you the principles — if there is any question you wish to ask we will be glad to answer it.

We all send you the Salutations of the New Year.

Very sincerely your friend
Anna Spafford

Mrs. Gould, who with Mrs. Lee stayed with you at Germantown, wishes to be remembered to you.

The picture I sent you showing part of the city wall and a section of the houses in Jerusalem shows as the highest house within the walls, one of the houses we occupy.

It is difficult for me to go into details respecting this work, for I could fill volumes. I have tried to give you the principles—if there is any question you wish to ask we will be glad to answer it.

We all send you the salutations of the New Year.

Very sincerely, your friend
Anna Spafford

Read More About It

General Works on Women in the Holiness Movement

Epstein, Barbara L.
  1981   *The Politics of Domesticity: Women, Evangelism, and Temperance in Nineteenth-Century America.* Middletown, CT: Wesleyan University Press.

Hardesty, Nancy, Lucille Sider Dayton, and Donald Dayton
  1979   "Women in the Holiness Movement: Feminism in the Evangelical Tradition." In *Women of Spirit: Female Leadership in the Jewish and Christian Traditions*, ed., Rosemary Ruether and Eleanor McLaughlin. New York: Simon and Schuster, 242-244.

Scanzoni, Letha Dawson and Susan Settag
  1981   "Women in Evangelical Holiness, and Pentecostal Traditions." In *Women and Religion in America*, ed., Rosemary Radford Ruether and Rosemary Skinner Keller, 3 vols. San Francisco: Harper and Rowe, 3:223-225.

Stanley, Susie
  1987   *Alma White: Holiness Preacher with a Feminist Message.* Ph.D. Dissertation, University of Denver.

  1989   "Empowered Foremothers, Wesleyan/Holiness Women Speak to Today's Christian Feminists," *Wesleyan Theological Journal* 103-116.

Works on Specific Women Mentioned

Barry, Kathleen
> 2000   *Susan B. Anthony: A Biography of a Singular Feminist.* Bloomington, IN: First Books Library.

Bordin, Ruth
1986   *Frances Willard: A Biography.* Chapel Hill, NC: University of North Carolina Press.

First, Ruth and Ann Scott
> 1990   *Olive Schreiner.* New Brunswick, NJ: Rutgers University Press.

Geniesse, Jane Fletcher
> 2008   *American Priestess: The Extraordinary Story of Anna Spafford and the American Colony in Jerusalem.* New York, NY: Doubleday.

Horowitz, Helen Lefkowitz
> 1994   *The Power and Passion of M. Carey Thomas.* New York, NY: Knopf.

Mathers, Helen
> 2014   *Patron Saint of Prostitutes: Josephine Butler and a Victorian Scandal.* Gloucestershire, UK: The History Press.

Mathes, Valerie Sherer
> 2012   *Divinely Guided: The California Work of the Women's National Indian Association* (the group founded by Amelia Stone Quinton). Lubbock, TX: Texas Tech University Press.

Mitchell, Sally
> 2004   *Frances Power Cobbe: Victorian Feminist, Journalist, Reformer.* Charlottesville, VA: University of Virginia Press.

Moyle, Franny
    2014 *Constance: The Tragic and Scandalous Life of Mrs. Oscar Wilde.* New York, NY: Pegasus Books.

Pryor, Elizabeth Brown
    1988 Clara Barton, Professional Angel. Philadelphia, PA: University of Pennsylvania Press.

Smith, Amanda and Bishop Thoburn
    An Autobiography. The Story of the Lord's Dealings with Mrs. Amanda Smith: The Colored Evangelist, Containing and Account of Her Life Work of Faith, and Her Travels in America, England, Ireland, Scotland, India, and Africa, as an Independent Missionary. First Fruits Press: http://place.asburyseminary.edu/firstfruitsheritagematerial/139/

Works on Hannah Whitall Smith

Henry, Marie
    1984 *The Secret Life of Hannah Whitall Smith.* Grand Rapids, MI: Chosen Books Publishing Co.

    1993 *Hannah Whitall Smith.* Grand Rapids, MI: Bethany House Publishers.

Meneghel, Meg A.
    2000 *Becoming a "Heretic": Hannah Whitall Smith, Quakerism, and the Nineteenth-Century Holiness Movement.* Ph.D. Thesis, Indiana University.

Parker, Robert Allerton
    1960 *A Family of Friends: The Story of the Transatlantic Smiths.* London: Museum Press.

Strachey, Ray

> 1914 *A Quaker Grandmother: Hannah Whitall Smith*. New York, NY: Fleming H. Revell.

Works by Hannah Whitall Smith

> 1875 *The Christian's Secret to a Happy Life*. First Fruits Press: http://place.asburyseminary.edu/firstfruitsheritagematerial/146/

> 1878 *Bible Readings: On the Progressive Development of Truth and Experience in the Books of the Old Testament.* First Fruits Press: http://place.asburyseminary.edu/firstfruitsheritagematerial/149/

> 1893 *Everyday Religion; or, The Common-sense Teaching of the Bible*

> 1903 *The Unselfishness of God and How I Discovered It.* First Fruits Press: http://place.asburyseminary.edu/firstfruitsheritagematerial/148/

> 1906 *The God of All Comfort and the Secret of His Comforting.* First Fruits Press: http://place.asburyseminary.edu/firstfruitsheritagematerial/147/

> 1928 *Religious Fanaticism: Extracts From the Papers of Hannah Whitall Smith*. Edited with an Introduction by Ray Strachey. Faber and Gwyer Limited: London.

> 1949 *A Religious Rebel: The Letters of "H.W.S."* (Mrs. Pearsall Smith). Edited by her son Logan Pearsall Smith. London, Nisbet.

> 1950 *Philadelphia Quaker: The Letters of Hannah Whitall Smith*. Edited by her son Logan Pearsall Smith. New York, NY: Harcourt, Brace

www.ingramcontent.com/pod-product-compliance
Lightning Source LLC
Chambersburg PA
CBHW060235050426
42448CB00009B/1452